Jean -

I'm so glad this year and New Orleans brought us back together again. Thanks for the love, the laughs, all your

In Search of My Father

support. I can't wait to collaborate on all the projects we can think of. Your greatest wealth is your most kind heart. The one who is worthy will always honor that. XOXO, S

This book is a memoir. I have tried to recreate events, locales and conversations from my memories of them. In order to maintain their anonymity in some instances, I have changed the names of individuals and places; I may have changed some identifying characteristics and details such as physical properties, occupations and places of residence.

ISBN 0-9844233-8-9
EAN-13 978-0-9844233-8-5
LCCN 2011942281

In Search of My Father

A Memoir By

Shadé Ashani

Edited by Bianca Philippi

Your Time Publishing, LLC P.O. Box 872365 New Orleans, Louisiana 70187

Aeneas carried his aged father on his back from the ruins of Troy and so do we all, whether we like it or not, perhaps even if we have never known them. --Angela Carter

I cannot think of any need in childhood as strong as the need for a father's protection. --Freud

For Shannon

To my Aunt Virginia, thank you for saving my life.

To Olivia Olakunmi, Bunmi and Temilade, I love you endlessly.
To Akin, you'll always be a reminder to me that God is real.
To my mom, thank you for always believing in me.
To Justus, I love you with all my heart.

"This book causes me to acknowledge my pain, feel a kinship and oneness to my fellow humans while a divine spirit from within and on high, heals and strengthens me. Precious angel, with all my heart, I thank you and give thanks for you. Please continue to live your destiny." -my sister, Olivia Olakunmi.

Dear Daddy,

I have not much to thank you for it seems. But I am grateful that you told me I was beautiful enough times as a child to make me believe it. Your words were somehow engrained in my head. So much so that when I look in the mirror sometimes to this day I hear your voice play in my head, as if seeing my reflection begins a recording in my subconscious, "My beautiful little girl. You are--hold your head high--you are a royal descendant of the Yoruba tribe. A real princess." I hope you knew that I never hated you, Daddy. I was disappointed. I stopped talking to you not to hurt you, but to protect myself. I was tired of the lies. Rest in Peace knowing that I forgive you.

Preface

According to the U.S. Census Bureau, 24 million children in America, approximately one out of every three, live in a home without their biological father. Consequently there is what the National Fatherhood Initiative has named the "father factor" in a myriad of social issues including poverty, maternal and child health, incarceration, crime, teen pregnancy, child abuse, drug and alcohol abuse, education, and childhood obesity. *

Children in father-absent homes are five times more likely to be poor. In 2002, 7.8 percent of children in married-couple families were living in poverty, compared to 38.4 percent of children in female-householder families. Source: U.S. Census Bureau, Children's Living Arrangements and Characteristics: March 2002, P200-547, Table C8. Washington D.C.: GPO, 2003.

A child with a nonresident father is 54 percent more likely to be poorer than his or her father. Source: Sorenson, Elaine and Chava Zibman. "Getting to Know Poor Fathers Who Do Not Pay Child Support." Social Service Review 75 (September 2001): 420-434.

A study of 3,400 middle schoolers indicated that not living with both biological parents quadruples the risk of having an affective disorder. Source: Cuffe, Steven P., Robert E. McKeown, Cheryl L. Addy, and Carol Z. Garrison. "Family Psychosocial Risk Factors in a Longitudinal Epidemiological Study of Adolescents." Journal of American Academic Child Adolescent Psychiatry 44 (February 2005): 121-129.

Even after controlling for income, youths in father-absent households still had significantly higher odds of incarceration than those in mother-father families. Youths who never had a father in the household experienced the highest odds. Source: Harper, Cynthia C. and Sara S. McLanahan. "Father Absence and Youth Incarceration." Journal of Research on Adolescence 14 (September 2004): 369-397.

A study of 13,986 women in prison showed that more than half grew up without their father. Forty-two percent grew up in a single-mother household and sixteen percent lived with neither parent. Source: Snell, Tracy L and Danielle C. Morton. Women in Prison: Survey of Prison Inmates, 1991. Bureau of Justice Statistics Special Report. Washington, DC: US Department of Justice, 1994: 4.

Even after controlling for community context, there is significantly more drug use among children who do not live with their mother and father. Source: Hoffmann, John P. "The Community Context of Family Structure and Adolescent Drug Use." Journal of Marriage and Family 64 (May 2002): 314-330.

In a study of INTERPOL crime statistics of 39 countries, it was found that single parenthood ratios were strongly correlated with violent crimes. This was not true 18 years ago. Source: Barber, Nigel. "Single Parenthood As a Predictor of Cross-National Variation in Violent Crime." Cross-Cultural Research 38 (November 2004): 343-358.

Being raised by a single mother raises the risk of teen pregnancy, marrying with less than a high school degree, and forming a marriage where both partners have less than a high school degree. Source: Teachman, Jay D. "The Childhood Living Arrangements of Children and the Characteristics of Their Marriages." Journal of Family Issues 25 (January 2004): 86-111.

Researchers using a pool from both the U.S. and New Zealand found strong evidence that father absence has an effect on early sexual activity and teenage pregnancy. Teens without fathers were twice as likely to be involved in early sexual activity and seven times more likely to get pregnant as an adolescent. Source: Ellis, Bruce J., John E. Bates, Kenneth A. Dodge, David M. Ferguson, L. John Horwood, Gregory S. Pettit, and Lianne Woodward. "Does Father Absence Place Daughters at Special Risk for Early Sexual Activity and Teenage Pregnancy." Child Development 74 (May/June 2003): 801-821.

Compared to living with both parents, living in a single-parent home doubles the risk that a child will suffer physical, emotional, or educational neglect. Source: America's Children: Key National Indicators of Well-Being. Table SPECIAL1. Washington, D.C.: Federal Interagency Forum on Child and Family Statistics, 1997.

The National Longitudinal Survey of Youth found that obese children are more likely to live in father-absent homes than are non-obese children. Source: National Longitudinal Survey of Youth

Fatherless children are twice as likely to drop out of school. Source: U.S. Department of Health and Human Services. National Center for Health Statistics. Survey on Child Health. Washington, D.C.: GPO, 1993.

Students living in father-absent homes are twice as likely to repeat a grade in school; 10 percent of children living with both parents have never repeated a grade, compared to 20 percent of children in stepfather families and 18 percent in mother-only families. Source: Nord, Christine Winquist, and Jerry West. Fathers' and Mothers' Involvement in Their Children's Schools by Family Type and Resident Status. (NCES 2001-032). Washington, D.C.: U.S. Department of Education, National Center for Education Statistics, 2001.

A study of 156 victims of child sexual abuse found that the majority of the children came from disrupted or single-parent homes; although stepfamilies make up only about 10 percent of all families, 27 percent of the abused children lived with either a stepfather or the mother's boyfriend. Source: Beverly Gomes-Schwartz, Jonathan Horowitz, and Albert P. Cardarelli, "Child Sexual Abuse Victims and Their Treatment," U.S. Department of Justice, Office of Juvenile Justice and Delinquency Prevention.

Fatherless children are at greater risk of suicide. Source: U.S. Department of Health and Human Services, National Center for Health Statistics, Survey on Child Health, Washington, DC, 1993.

We may not be able to control for the father factor entirely, but we can begin to acknowledge the severity of the impact father absence is having on children and their development and respond. As we work to better society through federal and social programs, non-profit organization efforts, and perhaps most importantly, as individuals, we must take the importance of fathers into account. There is an undeniable interrelatedness between many social issues and I wonder how large a role father absence plays in those connections and in possibly confounding other studies. While the cycle of poverty and broken families cannot be solely blamed on an absent father, until we decide that it is absolutely unacceptable for a father to abandon his children and that decision is reflected from our laws to our dining tables, we will continue to see the far-reaching effects of father absence. This book aims to ask, using my life as an example of these effects, is fatherlessness an aspect of humanity that we are willing to accept? If we must accept that there will always be varying degrees of fatherlessness, what can we realistically do to prevent the trauma from radiating out across society?

*Statistics can be found at the National Fatherhood Initiative

This is my life as I remember it. My reality, my distorted perspective through the lens of trauma. My sparkling joys and darkest, most painful miseries. My secrets and my fall from grace into a rape treatment facility and the unbelievably difficult climb through depression and anorexia back to self-love and faith. My father used to say that there simply isn't enough time in life to make all the mistakes in the world ourselves; we must learn from each other if we wish to advance as a human race. In response, I offer, *In Search of My Father*, hoping that others might be able to see themselves in me, accept their fathers even sooner than I did and truly heal. We can't love anyone, surely not ourselves, until we do. This is my story and above all else, the truth of a broken little girl who grew into a compassionate young woman—one who spent far too much time in search of her father.

Introduction

Our bodies betray us constantly, from head colds to stomach cramps to breast cancer. Our society accepts this and responds accordingly. Advil and Midol pass through the FDA with flying colors and support groups are formed, filled with pink-ribbon sporting bald women. But when our minds betray us, people are less sympathetic. There aren't any walk-a-thons for postpartum depression or star-studded galas for schizos. There's something dark, shameful and secretive about being mentally "unhealthy." We rip the labels off our anti-depressants and therapist visits are called fruitless shopping trips. We should be able to control our minds, our thoughts. Relinquishing that control by admitting that sometimes our thoughts are not our own is far too terrifying. But our minds do betray us.

I've laughed hysterically at the sight of a crow being blazed over by a semi-truck and wept openly watching *The Sound of Music*. Where do you go when you can't count on your brain to respond to your surroundings? Your former safe haven becomes a scary place. Your day dreams, your thoughts, your hopes are not your own. New serrated kitchen knife. My forearms will be no match. Box of Raisin Bran. Maybe I'll eat the whole box and throw it up. Failed bio quiz. I'm useless and stupid. I should do the world a favor and die already. Everything seemed backwards and the only things I could count on to recreate the same emotion were the clouds.

I was just a little speck underneath their incredible kingdom. I'd lay there and watch the fluffy shapes float by amazed at their vastness and assured of my insignificance. When I was a little girl, I used to love to discover shapes, animals, faces in the clouds. "There's a dragon blowing smoke out his nose!" I'd screech and tug on the pant leg of whoever was nearest.

But there were no clouds in the sky that day.

I noticed this as the smell of my searing flesh filled my nostrils and I choked back gags. A few hundred yards away from Union Station in South Central Los Angeles, my naked body was strewn across the scorched iron train tracks in desperate hopes of being run over, brutally severed and decapitated. I had strategically placed myself around a bend in the tracks so the conductor would have no choice but to murder me.

He would see me, my neck delicately placed over the guiding metal, my head resting on a back pack filled with championship basketball t-shirts and fervently blow his whistle in a futile attempt to make me love life enough to move. I crossed my arms over my chest, encircling my neck with my hands. I imagined I would be strong, stubborn, removed, but I gulped as I tried to picture my head separated, rolling, and then coming to rest amongst the soda cans, used syringes, and pre-op transsexual hooker newspaper ads behind me.

My mind started racing. Who would find my body? Perhaps the conductor whom I had forced into becoming my only witness would tremble into the station and tell someone where to find my remains. He would be too queasy, knowing what the powerful wheels had done when matched against my vertebrae. Perhaps a maintenance man would stumble across my midsection, vomit at the gruesome sight and continue to dry heave, fingers shaking, as he tried to call the police.

Would my mother have to identify me? Would she able to?

"Yes, that is my daughter's belly button."

No, she would have to be strong, squeeze the circulation in my Aunt Virginia's hand to a halt as the medical examiner pulled back a curtain revealing the reassembled pieces of her first child's maimed corpse.

She would scream; she would cry, but she would live. I, thankfully, would not.

But, what about my soul? My skin started crawling. Where would it go? Would it flow right out of my trunk riding along like a raft on a river of my blood? When my dejected spirit hit the air, the angels would see my anguish, sympathize with my torture. Surely, God took mercy on the souls of the slaves who threw themselves overboard into the freezing Atlantic and on the Jews who shot themselves, having grown tired of playing the most sadistic game of hide and seek. Yes, of course my angels would understand, take my broken heart into their arms and speak for me when anti-suicide whispers filled the heavenly courtroom on my Judgment Day.

"She was a good girl, Father," my angel would say. "She was lost and we could not save her, Lord." No response.

"She was very faithful in the past," she would offer feebly.

"And then you abandoned me!" I would violently interject, accusing God.

My angel would hang her head.

"Didn't you remember? Weren't you watching?" I shouted, hot tears running down my face, my whole being shaking.

"I was the one. Who loved you. Who trusted you." I pressed on the words that made my voice crack and shake.

"I was the little girl who rode her bike," I sputtered. "Two miles! Getting my Sunday dress caught in the spokes to come to Your house while my whole family slept in. Weren't you paying attention?"

No response.

I was incredulous now, hysterical. All my hard work, my obedience, and the connection I thought we shared was for naught. I collapsed before God's feet while my angel looked pitifully on.

"How could you leave me? How could you? How could you?"

I sobbed uncontrollably.

"My child, I never left you nor forsook you."

"And I'm not finished with you."

I lifted my head.

A whistle sounded in the distance. The click-clack of the train switching tracks to make the sudden turn I had hidden myself around. A hawk had started circling over my head. A single cloud floated by. A gold fish.

I gathered my knees to my chest and lifted myself up and over the tracks. My toes were only centimeters from the rusted metal. The whistle grew louder and louder as the ground beneath me shook. Sharp rocks and wood chips around me danced. The train was so close now that I could see the conductor's little blue hat. I screamed into the wind as the force of the passing train knocked me over backwards. I kept screaming as the air brutally whipped over my cuts and burns. I felt the thick consistency of blood in my throat. The last cars passed and I realized that my mouth was open, I was pushing, but no sound was coming out.

I stood up and watched the caboose pull into the station. Putting my clothes back on proved a difficult task with my burns but I managed. I tried to whimper but my voice was gone. I would continue with my plan I decided, slinging my backpack over one un-hurt shoulder. I slowly made my way towards the station. I had chickened out of suicide.

Back to Plan A.

My plan to run away from home was only a day old, but I liked it well enough. It provided me with two essentials for happiness: it got me out of Santa Clarita and away from my family.

One

My mother, Alison Joy Cecilia, was born to Anthony and Louise Stec. They were a loving middle class couple of Polish descent who never missed mass on Sundays. Living up to her middle name, Alison Joy was a happy-go-lucky, freckly and friendly child who was always smiling. By high school, she was so smart, pretty and popular that as I looked through the yearbook to see all the pages my mother graced, I wondered if we would have been friends had we gone to school together. Staring at her straight white teeth and smooth skin, she was almost overwhelming in her perfection.

After skipping a grade, she graduated at seventeen and applied to her dream school, the University of Washington. When her father died, she decided to study close to home in Los Angeles. It was at UCLA's prestigious film school where she would meet and fall in love with a tall, dark, and handsome Nigerian man who graduated with a Bachelor's from the University of Washington.

The year my mother applied to the University of Washington, my father graduated from their undergraduate school; he then transferred to get to the best film school on the west coast and as destiny would have it, my mother. He wistfully remembered the times before he had the courage to talk to her; the way she smiled and laughed with her friends, the way her long reddish hair flowed out behind her in the wind as she jetted around UCLA's hilly campus on a moped.

Isn't it amazing, magical even, the way our worlds collide?

The philosopher Virgil said, "Wherever the fates lead us, let us follow." I'd like to think my parents were destined to be together and that I, their first daughter, was meant to write this book.

When I was in the eighth grade, my father decided he was going to Nigeria for six months; it would be almost six years before I ever spent longer than two weeks at a time with him again. He took my self-esteem with him to that faraway place. Over time, the anger that I originally felt towards him for leaving turned inward; "why isn't he here?" eventually became "what did I do to make him go?" I figured I wasn't enough. I wasn't good enough or beautiful enough or smart enough for him to stay. Instead of watching me grow up, he would rather be a hemisphere away in a third world country, catching malaria and living in a crappy apartment. He would endure anything to be away from me. I hated him for leaving. But not as much as I hated myself.

I find it no coincidence that I got my first boyfriend three months after he left. I realize now that my interactions with men were completely centered around filling the role of a father in my life. I didn't want sex or romance; I just wanted someone to call me and ask how my day went, if I had gotten any test scores back, how my friends were doing. I wanted someone to find me interesting.

Very quickly I found out that if I wanted that kind of attention from a man, I would have to make sacrifices. I lost all sense of who I was, validating myself in dysfunctional encounters with men. Frozen in my trauma, I kept attracting the same men: the same mean, insecure, jealous, emotionally abusive men over and over again. For some unfortunate reason, the universe has decided that the match for a girl with a Daddy abandonment complex is a nearly psychotically possessive, control-freak. Looking back, I know I was searching for my father in boys who could never replace him, boys who were just as sick I was.

I was struggling to find a definition of myself without the man who helped to build my identity. Who was I, if not my Daddy's girl? Was I no longer the cherished jewel he told me I was? Had I done something to lose the title? My entire existence was in question in his absence. Whose was I, if he wouldn't claim me?

Two

"Who are they to you? Those peasants aren't worthy to sit next to YOU at the lunch table. They don't own that lunch table. Next time they ask you how your skin got to be brown you tell them it is so because you're a REAL African princess. As a matter of fact, I'll buy you that forsaken lunch table."

I absorbed my father's words as the tears dried on my cheeks and hot pink Lion King T-shirt. Another day in the 3rd grade. Another day of deflecting racist comments from my classmates.

"Were you in a fire?"

"Have you ever tried really scrubbing? Like super hard?"

I repeated their cruel words to my father, using an exaggerated, mimicking voice in an attempt to remove their venom. No such luck. I burst into tears afresh.

"Don't cry please, Ashani," my father demanded firmly yet kindly all at once.

I took one last meaningful sniff as he took my hand. For as long as I can remember my father and I held hands almost everywhere we went. We lived in Santa Clarita, California and to say my West African imported father and his Velcro attached light brown daughter stood out would have been an understatement. In 1992, Santa Clarita was a collection of disturbingly similar towns in suburban California where the cool kids wore the same skater brands, had the same porcupine-inspired haircuts spiked and gelled into place, and drove the same types of cars, gargantuan sports utility vehicles. A Pleasantville of Caucasian clones with a sprinkling of illegal Mexican immigrants for household help would summarize it best in my opinion. I often figured Santa Clarita to be a place where white people escaped the "trauma" of all that danged diversity in big city Los Angeles 40 miles south.

Why would my very interracially married parents choose Santa Clarita of all places, to raise their two mixed kids? Something about good schools or a bigger house. I have no idea. I always tuned it out whenever my mother tried to justify to me why I had to be socially electrocuted every day.

I was seven years old when we moved from East Los Angeles to my own personal hell. And thus began my life as "other." Some of my first conscious memories are of my father telling me that I was different, special, incredible, intelligent, even wise. My middle name, Ashani, translates to "a special person" in Yoruba. My father never called me anything else. Apparently, I wasn't meant to be one of the clones. I remember the way he used to look at me then. Perhaps love isn't even the right word to describe the way he beheld me as a child. I think now it was awe, which I mirrored back to him. I was a Daddy's girl through and through.

"Daddy, can we get ice cream please?" I asked as we made our way out of our museum-esque home to the car.

We passed my mother's Kenyan gallery of photographs with overhead lighting in the hall. The sculptures on pedestals stood out in the sea of cream carpet and black leather couches. I reached for his hand, knowing he'd never say no regardless of how perilously close it was to dinner time.

He smiled, "We'll see."

I climbed into the front seat even though mom wanted me to ride in back. Daddy always let me break the rules. We never discussed it, but we both secretly took pleasure in disobeying her in these minuscule ways. Today I wouldn't beg him to home school me I decided. I didn't have the energy. It was the only time his "we'll see" actually meant "no" and it broke my heart.

We pulled up to a red light and the diesel engine of the Mercedes shook my whole little body. It was a soft yet unsubtle rumble that made you feel like if you closed your eyes you could just disappear into the roar. I opened my tightly sealed brown eyes, disappointed to see I had not gained the ability to float away and looked around at Lyon's Avenue, the main drag through town. I felt nauseous as I took in the endless line of raised, lifted, or otherwise tricked out pickup trucks in front of us.

My dad pointed to a man with his finger up his nose next to us and I burst out laughing. The sound caught awkwardly in my throat at first. I had been holding a knot there since 8:30 that morning, but soon the chuckle gained momentum. I started making faces at the man digging for gold in the side view mirror and my dad joined in the fun. Soon we were in stitches. When the man found whatever treasure he was searching for and held it up for examination, my dad dramatically feigned gagging and blazed through the red light, eyes wide, cheeks puffed, and tires squealing. People were honking at us, but this was before red light cameras so he just honked back a little melody and laughed even harder.

I caught his sidewise glance, mischievous glint and all, and felt the horror of the day slip away. When we were together, we were different, special, incredible together. Whatever oppressive loneliness I had felt would lift off my bones and let me dance again.

He popped in a Bob Marley's Greatest Hits cassette as we cruised along for what seemed like hours. "....*Cuz every little thing's gonna be alright.*" For the first time all day, it was. I was high on how much he loved me and only tomorrow could bring me down. "Monife', Babami," I said, reaching into the Styrofoam cup that held our two shared scoops of mint chocolate chip. I giggled when he scrunched his nose as I sloppily fed him an extra large spoonful. "Monife', omomi" he repeated with his mouth full, "I love you, my child."

"Too... many... chips," he struggled to chew and pretended to choke. He let go of the steering wheel and signaled for me to handle the navigating. I squealed, fighting back a grin, "Daddy! Daddy! You have to drive! I don't know how!" He nodded to me, as if to say, "You can do it." I pulled myself over the center console to share his seat with him. I and my Daddy's knees drove us home that day and there was only him and I in the whole world.

When I was born, my father was married to my mother. He was previously divorced, had impregnated two ex-girlfriends and had four children, one for each woman--one who none of my family would know existed until after his death.

Strange and gut wrenching family secrets are a part of being an Ogunleye family member it seems.

I was finishing the third grade when he told me I had two half-sisters. When I asked why he wasn't honest with me about my sisters from the beginning, he said he did it to protect me. From what? I wondered. Wouldn't that simply have been our reality? My other siblings would come over all the time. We'd go to each other's birthday parties and we would have all grown up together. Why wasn't that an option?

I figure he did it to preserve my opinion of him and to protect himself from the drama. He was never sued for back child support and he rarely paid it. My brother and I never wanted for anything. Unfortunately, I cannot say the same for my sisters. My mother was the family's primary source of income; she made the rules and ran the show. His children, apparently, were his responsibility. She said she assumed he was taking care of his obligations to his other children and that was all I ever heard on the subject.

My mother was working seemingly constantly so I had only my father to scrutinize regarding the subject. Who were these siblings of mine? Where were they? What were they like? The pedestal my father placed himself on in my eyes began to crumble. My sisters were teenagers, six and eight years my senior when they were introduced to me as such, and the worst part was I already knew one of them.

She had been coming over for play dates. My father told me her mother was a co-worker and that it would be nice of me to play with her daughter.

The first time I remember meeting Bunmi I was 4 or 5 and we didn't get along. I couldn't figure out why my parents wanted me to play with her. She was too much older than me. She didn't want to play with any of my toys or with me. Her lackluster enthusiasm for playing with my beloved Barbies sent me right into a tantrum. I remember thinking she was mean. We'd play tag and she'd whomp me too hard on the arm. It breaks my heart now to think of how bratty I was to her. The times she bit her tongue when I screeched out "I'm going to tell my Daddy on you!"

She must have wanted to sprint her eleven year old legs passed me and yell, "He was my Daddy first!" over her shoulder. But that guilt for her pain isn't mine to bear. I can only imagine how I would've treated her if I had known the truth. I believe I would have loved her then as much as I do now.

Later, Bunmi showed me pictures of us together when I was a baby. Neither of my parents had ever talked to me about her. I was shocked.

29

Who told me what and when on the subject of my sisters is a bit blurry for me. Deciphering all the lies from the truth would occupy my time for years in therapy later and I often found that I flat out don't remember large chunks of time in my childhood. Yet, I remember the year I turned nine vividly. It was the year I was forgotten. It was the year I disappeared within myself, creating my own world, where only my truth existed. I began journaling as an outlet. I wrote short stories, plays, and hundreds of letters to my sisters that I never sent. Despite barely knowing them, I felt bonded to them in the trauma these crazy adults were putting us through.

Besides having two new teenaged sisters, our home was being remodeled and we were surviving in what some might describe as a refugee camp. Blue tarps, omnipresent dust and debris, taped off zones, and ceaseless hammering/drilling/banging filled the halls. My beloved grandmother who helped raise me and who lived with us since I was born passed away. My younger brother's anti-seizure medication had not found a comfortable balance and we were in the emergency room more times than I could count. It was a hellaious, horrifying year full of darkness, fear, sirens, and white noise.

At night, the muffled wails and bellows of our parents came through the walls of the bedroom my brother and I shared. Akin crawled into my bunk, scared to the point of shaking. I did my best to comfort him back to sleep.

"It's ok, Akin," I whispered. "It'll be over soon."

"Why are they so mad?" Akin looked up at me, trembling and clutching one of my stuffed animals to his chest. He only had the use of one arm and the other would spasm when he was under stress. I had to maneuver myself to be on his left side or I ran the risk of being smacked all night.

"I don't know," I said and put the headphones to my cassette-playing walkman in his ears.

30

"Just try to relax," I offered.
"Huh?" He couldn't hear me over Brandy's debut album.
I shook my head, "Nothing."

"Just try to relax," I said again aloud. This time to myself, but it offered me no comfort. Mom and Dad are getting worse, I thought, as what sounded like a dresser drawer or filing cabinet boomed to the floor.

They almost always fought in the middle of the night. Akin and I were supposed to pretend like nothing had happened the next day, but Daddy didn't come down stairs to see us off to school when they fought like that. It was strange to eat breakfast in silence while the remnants of their marriage hung in the air.

I learned how to tune out that year, a survival tool I used for years to come. To this day, if someone is speaking and I don't want to hear what they're saying, I can go somewhere in my head, think of a place I'd rather be and literally not hear a single word the person is saying. Maybe living in a fishbowl would be similar with no day particularly discernible from the next. I existed in my head and was happiest alone in peace.

But I was not a hermit child. On the contrary, I was on the swim team during the summer, a member of Girl Scout Troop 643, started oil painting lessons, piano lessons, was first chair flute in my elementary school's orchestra, went to horseback riding camp, ran track on the city-wide team that met at the local community college, and had a math tutor who also taught me to roller blade, crochet, and make beaded jewelry. My mother wanted me to be exposed to the world, to be cultured, to be geared towards the college bound track for success. The fact that I still had baby teeth was totally irrelevant. Much of my work ethic, drive, and desire to be busy comes from her.

As I got older, I came to realize I was given a very privileged childhood. My mother orchestrated an amazing life for me, and I never wanted for anything save for her attention. Constant household help from assistants, babysitters, and the Nanas ran our house like a ship. My mother was Captain. There were many Nanas over the years, more than I care to try to remember. Their job was truly brutal. On their shoulders the brunt of home life fell: cooking, cleaning, grocery shopping, taking care of Akin, making all of our lunches for the day, trash cans, laundry, and dog duty. The list of their responsibilities was never quite finished and I felt sorry for them.

Akin was such a nightmare back then, prone to crying, screaming, hitting fits and temper tantrums so intense you thought he was joking at first. He's not actually lying on the floor at the supermarket in this small town and clearing off full shelves in the cereal aisle because you told him he can't have Coco Crispy Puffs, is he? Oh, yes. Yes, he is. He's choking while screeching your name at the top his lungs, interjected with how much he hates you. And he'll probably try to kick or bite you if you touch him. Everyone is watching and the manager has come by to ask you to leave when you think, "The Civil War in El Salvador is better than this." God bless our Nanas. Anyone who stayed over a month got my respect.

One afternoon, I overheard Nana saying a Santeria prayer of exorcism over Akin while he napped. He was like a little demon half the time so I didn't stop her. Western medicine had failed him so far so why not? He was always angry. But hey, a mild case of cerebral palsy, epilepsy, ADHD, mental retardation, and no real possibility of an independent future might piss you off that much too.

Akin's health or lack thereof was like a raincloud over all of our lives—you never knew when lightening would strike. I was scared for him. I resented him. I just wanted him to be ok.

To my parents, raising Akin seemed to be an afterthought to simply keeping him alive. Disciplining him was an issue on which they never quite reached a consensus. My father was far stricter with him and refused to listen to or believe anything the doctors said regarding Akin's developmental capabilities. He was to be treated like any other Nigerian son and my father never gave up hope that Akin would be miraculously healed. In contrast, my mother was sympathetic to and realistic about Akin's struggles.

If you were Akin, who would you want to be around? Yeah, mom was the obvious choice for his fave. I couldn't really blame him either, but I was just a kid so I did. I also blamed my mother for babying him and turning him into a spoiled brat.

Harsh as that may sound I didn't feel like I knew my mother well enough to understand her thinking when it came to raising Akin. We didn't spend much one on one time together when I was very young. Mostly, I remember feeling annoyed that her free time for parenting was taken up by Akin's ceaseless health problems.

As the responsible parent with no real support from her spouse, I'm sure she felt trapped by the mortgage, Akin's medical bills, and the need to provide health insurance for all of us. You can imagine that this left little time for mother-daughter manicures. It saddens me to know the memories I treasure from my childhood with my father were made possible because he was unemployed and refused to go to Akin's doctor appointments.

With no real free time, my mother's role in my life was mostly behind the scene. She worked from 3pm to 3am, an opposite schedule of the average kid. She was asleep as Akin and I got ready for school in the morning and gone to work by the time I came home from whatever practice/meeting/lesson I had been driven to and from by the sitter.

That same year my mom bought me a book about a girl with a younger disabled brother; I thought flippantly, if Akin was my only problem, I'd be fine. The moral of the story said to me: be understanding, patient, loving. Your brother needs your support because he's so sick and your parents have a lot on their plates with that. I hated that book.

33

"What about us?" I wanted to shout at that sissy, smiling sister on the cover. "What about when we have a bad day? What if I don't feel like sucking it up?"

Akin never, ever sucked it up for me. The more I stared at the cover, the angrier I became. There she was passively, sitting on the wayside, never speaking up about anything. And she had the audacity to smile? Why wasn't our pain relevant? Sure, I wasn't having a life-threatening Grand-Mal seizure once a week, but I had already done enough sucking it up for a third grader in my opinion.

Had my mother read the book and thought this would be helpful to me? Had she envisioned it would be comforting to me to know that there were other girls out there who had Nanas putting Barbie band-aids on their knee scrapes because their mothers were also running late to neurologist appointments downtown? Had she hoped I would find solace in knowing that the jealousy and frustration I felt towards the attention Akin's behavioral outbursts won him was normal? I felt nothing so soothing as all that. I tore the cover off so I wouldn't have to see that sissy's smiling face ever again and thanked my mom for the book later. I guess I had received the message after all, much to my chagrin.

I don't remember us having a discussion about the book, so I was left to assume her message was the one I had inferred. "Can you please just be ok? I don't really have the time or energy for you not to be." That message informed our every interaction. I'm sure that's not what she meant wholeheartedly but our communication was either nonexistent or untruthful as a result. I didn't feel like she was talking to me to get to know me or creating a relationship with me that made me feel like I could go to her. Our conversations were light, airy, and often brief. Maybe she assumed that my feelings on the subject of my brother's health couldn't be articulated at age nine.

But if ever there was a nine year old who could articulate such an emotion, it very well might have been me. For starters, her own mother had been reading to me and teaching me to read since I was a baby. I could speak both Spanish and English at around the same level by preschool. And my father was so distrusting of the California public school system that I had my own assignments and book reports to turn into him by the time second grade rolled around. Each morning I had to pick an LA Times cover story to read and then report to him the facts, followed by my opinion. I also had five vocabulary words to memorize and use in a sentence as I walked out the door. He would choose long, advanced words at random from some old British boarding school work book he had. He read them and their definitions to me in an exaggerated and terrible British accent.

I laughed then, but I loved the words: finicky, facetious, filament, finagle, feisty, fortitude. The extra letters rolled and ran, bounced and shivered across the pages I wrote them on in my best attempt at cursive. Their fanciful foreign appeal enraptured me. I cherished my extra dad-work notebooks. They were filled, practically bursting with his love for me.

He listened to my stories about mean girls at school, boring teachers, and hair woes. He consoled me, helped me put my Encyclopedia set to good use, and drove me to Crenshaw Blvd in Inglewood so a woman named Magic with fingernails longer than her fingers themselves and a chest tattoo could braid my hair. I felt invested in and adored. I felt smart, capable, like my opinions mattered.

We were halfway through Shakespeare's classics by the time my fifth grade class started reading *Romeo and Juliet*. It had been my very first Shakespeare two years earlier and I was obsessed with it. The drama. The romance. The anticipation and hopefulness of forbidden love. I recited one of Juliet's monologues for the class and sealed my fate as weird nerd brown girl with a showman's streak for all time. To my mother I may have been a little girl, but in my mind, I had big girl problems. My family was dysfunctional and I needed help dealing with it. A support group full of other smiling sissies who also simultaneously loved and hated their sick or disabled siblings would have gone a long way. I could have also used a counselor to help me cope with my grandmother's death and parents' theatrical reenactments of the Civil War in the middle of night. What really blows me away looking back now is why no one thought to suggest a family therapist who met with The Ogunleyes, including my new sisters, to assist us in the adjustment period.

Regardless of how far my parents' heads were in the sand, my mother scheduled out a great life for me instead of getting us help as a family. Perhaps she intended to shelter me from the chaos. Unfortunately, I felt very alone. I already loved my sisters desperately and couldn't figure out why we were being kept apart.

In spite of all these scheduled group activities, I still hadn't made any real friends. I felt like I had to be nice to the people who were nice to me because well, this is where we lived and the pickings were slim. Truth is I didn't like any of 'em.

Looking at pictures documenting the countless hours I spent with all those blonde little girls immediately reminds me of how I felt in those moments: lonely, weird, awkward. It's written all over my face. I don't belong. Please, someone get me out of here. My eyes tell an even darker story.

I think my mother assumed that I was doing well in school, bringing home ribbons and plaques from track, swimming, orchestra and could ride both Western and English so everything was perfect, right?

My mom always acknowledged my accomplishments. She was proud of me when I succeeded and I relished the time I spent on her lap showing her my winnings. I can't be too hard on her here because I think any mother with a full time job, a disabled son, and an unsupportive partner would've had trouble making the rounds to the overachiever whose only complaint appeared to be about needing new oil paints by the end of the week.

The years of my childhood I remember most were an uncomfortable, dizzying experience. Which way was up? Who was telling the truth? Was my brother going to be alright? When was I going to see my sisters again? Why didn't Daddy love Mommy anymore? I remember falling asleep many nights, confused and struggling to understand what on earth was going on with my family. But one night stands out from the blur.

Three

From the top bunk, I tried to count my blinks. Sleepless again. As I was swinging my legs over the little ladder that would have led me to a glass of milk and a few chapters in the latest Sweet Valley High library rental, my dad burst through the door. He looked frazzled, unsure of himself. He didn't speak, but I psychically knew to go to him.

He was in his usual matching striped pajama set and velvet robe. I stuck my hand in the pocket of his robe and looked up at his tired face. Something was definitely wrong. What time was it? Why wasn't he talking? I didn't speak either. Rain poured against the windows and thunder boomed.

"Your mother is downstairs," he began.

Akin was stirring and I realized lights were flashing in through the bedroom window. What was the ambulance for? Akin was in bed.

My father and I walked down the stairs together in silence. I had no idea what to expect, but for some reason I wasn't particularly nervous. I was feeling pretty numb those days anyway.

I saw two police officers in the doorway explaining something to my mother, who for some reason was facing the wall to her right instead of the door where they were standing. She turned around to sign something they handed her. And I could see she was wearing a neck brace. She tucked her hair behind her ear and I could tell from down the hall that her hands were shaking violently.

My dad left my side where he had been standing firmly rooted with me. He said something to the officers I couldn't hear. My mother and the officers had been talking for a few minutes now and I realized I couldn't understand any of it. It all sounded so garbled and far away. I was entranced. My mother was crying and mascara was streaked down her face like a tragic Halloween mask.

This is so weird, I remember thinking. My mother was always perfect. I never saw her first thing in the morning or when she was getting ready for bed. When she came to a flute recital or swim meet, her hair and make-up were always done to a tee. This was a jarring and alarming version of her. She was unraveled. Her eyes wild.

"Mommy's ok," she called to me.

I was appalled. Mommy was clearly not ok. What the hell was going on? She hugged me and told me to go back to sleep. I reached for her perfectly manicured hand. She moved her hand over mine and squeezed it too hard. She needed her space. I walked slowly up the stairs, sincerely confused. Akin whispered from the top of the stairs, "What's happening?"

"Nothing. Mommy's sad."

"What?!" To a momma's boy through and through, I said exactly the wrong thing.

"Mommy! Mommy!" Akin shouted. "Where are you?"

I heard my mother sniffle and attempt to collect herself.

"Mommy's right here."

"Are you ok?" He called dashing down the stairs.

"Mommy's fine." I could hear her teeth gritting.

I followed Akin back to the living room, filled with dread and curiosity all at once.

Akin took in the neck brace and her tear stained face and immediately began to cry.

We sat down and listened while she gave a PG version of what I would later learn was a car accident so brutal, she was blessed to be able to walk or live.

Suddenly, the mother who was so far away was home. All the time. She was in pain and her attempts to cover it up or keep us sheltered from her misery were futile. Her every movement, the look in her eyes radiated her complete devastation. She was overly, gratingly chipper and I mirrored that back to her.

"Swim practice was great, Mom! I'm getting so good at breast stroke. I'm so excited you're coming to the meet on Saturday. I'm gonna kick butt for you!"

"I'll bring my pom-poms, girlie!"

I really just wanted to bring her flowers and ask her how she was feeling today or if she had gotten any news back from the doctor. But I didn't think she wanted to discuss what it was like to transition from being a high-powered, Emmy nominated, Hollywood career girl to a permanently disabled physical therapy patient. We were on a two-way fake street headed nowhere.

With my father I let my hair down. I didn't feel rushed or like I could say the wrong thing. He was easy to talk to and he often spoke very candidly with me. Too candidly actually. I was in the first grade when he told me that he was staying married to my mother for me and that Akin was his mother's son, not his. Something made me reply, "I know." We were sitting on a ledge in front of the house and I could feel how much he didn't want to go back inside. I thought he did it for me, but in reality he didn't have a better plan yet. My mother's accident only made these inappropriate private conversations stranger and more frequent.

He was depressed and those childlike moments we shared became more rare as time went on. He was sleeping strange hours during the day. Sometimes I heard him crying and praying for strength in Yoruba. My heart went out to him. I knew he was cracking, but I didn't know what to do for him. When he called me into his room to say my mother was killing him and the stress of their relationship was bringing his blood pressure up so high he didn't think it would ever come down, I wasn't surprised. For me, our home had taken on an us vs. them feeling long ago. But now, it was war. Me and Dad vs. Mom and Akin.

I was being brainwashed to believe my mother was killing my Daddy and I was livid with her for it. This was all her fault.

My diary entries during these years are rife with accusations against her:

She was taking out her frustration on me.
Maybe if she would just be nice sometimes, Daddy wouldn't be so miserable.
Daddy liked me better than her.
Most of these words were my father's.

One of my father's favorite subjects was my mother. He spent hours drilling me with "hypothetical" scenarios, making sure I had answers that I presume were least like my mother's reactions. He told me that he was frightened of her, that he had never hit her and that if she ever told the police any such lie, I should know that she had done it to herself. He would give

42

examples of her mistreatment of him, make me take notes, and demand that I swear never to speak to my own husband that way. I was nine years old. He would lay his head in my lap when a particularly draining session was over and say softly, "It's not supposed to be like this, Ashani. I don't want you to think this is normal. It's not."

I thought, "I knew that" and petted his hair. I didn't realize how sick it all was until years later, how much he lied, how wrong he was about my mother. She was the reason I had any life at all, but I wouldn't know that until I was almost seventeen years old.

For the time being, my Daddy was slipping through my fingers and I blamed her.

The last years we lived as a family are a blur of his depression. His backstabbing diatribes against my mother were confusing to me. Why didn't he divorce her and take me to live in an apartment close to my sisters? Why wasn't he thinking up a plan for us?

Well, he was thinking up a plan. It just didn't have me in it.

He sued his employers, Pitney Bowes, for racial discrimination and won 11.1 million dollars. The winnings were reduced on appeal to a number that was never disclosed to me, but ultimately, he had his ticket out of dodge.

Within a year, he told my mother that he was working on a project in Nigeria and would need to live there off and on. Six months. That was the very first timeline he promised. He dragged that out until his death twelve years later. He never came home for good again.

When we dropped him off at the airport that first time, he held me desperately, frighteningly tight to him and whispered, "Everything she did to me, she'll do to you. I'm sorry." I knew my Daddy wasn't coming home again. I was in shock the entire forty five minute car ride home.

Four

I think I stayed in that numb state for a few years, stunned in disbelief. Watching my father fade into the crowd at LAX turned on an auto-pilot switch somewhere inside me. I figured I could go through the motions until he came back home.

There were plenty of events, ceremonies, graduations, basketball games, open houses, winter formals, and Christmases that he missed. There are countless family pictures that his face isn't in, but I missed him everyday, not only on the special days.

My room was across from his office. Sometimes I'd rummage through the closet and try to find things that smelled like him. I missed the sound of his voice, his laugh. Mornings were now quiet and uninspired. Akin and I ate cereal together in silence or watched cartoons, something my father had expressly forbidden. Who was going to stop us? Mom's body clock was still set for the late night news so there were no more motivational, loving send offs. No more proverbs and prayers to apply to my life. If I had a rough day at school, I'd think to myself, I'll just pretend he's there and talk out loud like he's in the room with me. I thought it was a great idea to help ease my loneliness. But as soon as I opened his office door, the weight of my miscalculation rushed my being. His absence crushed my sternum with a force I could never quite prepare myself for. He was really gone. I hugged one of his pillows to my aching chest. I didn't know what I was supposed to do with that reality.

We tried speaking sporadically over the years. Sometimes on

awkward speaker phone group calls with the whole family.

I had never expressly asked him to come back home. How could I when he told me that the stress of his marriage and the house nearly killed him? Our relationship was so much more than a small-talk-infested, five-minute phone call. I didn't want to interact with him in this absurd, dishonest way.

"School is fine."

"No, basketball doesn't start till winter."

"I don't want to play soccer."

"Who are you and what have you done with my Daddy?" I wanted to say. Since I didn't know how to articulate my disappointment in him, our conversations got shorter.

But I finally did get up the nerve to ask him to come home.

It was a Tuesday afternoon during my junior year of high school. I had been keeping a dark secret for over a year.

I was driving my best friend Kelly and I to her house since mine certainly wasn't an option for studying.

"I'm leaving," I stated flatly over the Red Hot Chili Peppers song blaring through my speakers. Kelly turned it down.

"You're what?" she said in disbelief.

"You heard me," I bit back, agitated, but not at her.

"But where are you gonna go?"

"I want to be with horses," I said, thinking out loud. "So maybe somewhere in the country, but with a city somewhat close by...I

46

don't know..."

"But, Day," Kelly tried to joke. "You know they don't like your people in the country."

"I'd just be a farm hand or something," I shrugged. "No need to dislike a Negro who knows her place."

Kelly sighed, "I guess so."

We rode in silence until her driveway.

Kelly jumped out of the car and slammed the door with a bang.

"What're you gonna do about money? Food? What if you get fired from this stupid farmhand job?" She was yelling now.

"Kelly," I said.

"What if someone hurts you? Or something happens to you?"

"Kelly."

"Things go wrong you know! Just because you're smart doesn't mean you can handle yourself out there."

"Kelly, I..."

"And am I supposed to keep quiet? Because I don't think I can do that. No, no, no I won't keep quiet. You're my best friend."

Kelly eventually stopped, tears welling in her eyes.

"Kelly."

"What?"

"I can't do this anymore."

She searched my face.

"I know."

"Can we go inside now?" I pleaded, fidgeting in her grandiose circular driveway. I felt like the neighborhood was watching.

We walked around the bend created by a rather ridiculously Greek-themed fountain. The sunlight caught the concern in her light brown eyes.

Kelly was half Guyanese and half Irish. We bonded on our dual cultures, dual lives. It was hard enough to be mixed in the world, let alone Santa Clarita. We clung to each other. People accused us of being lesbians. I remember feeling upset until I realized that I wasn't even remotely interested in anyone at my school.

"Hi, Mom," Kelly and I said in unison as her mom limped passed us. She had a bad knee. I closed the door behind us and we beelined for her room.

"So should we do chem or calc homework first?"

I glared.

"Ok, ok." Kelly threw up her hands, "What's your plan?"

I hopped in front of her computer and started thinking of a good place to get lost.

"I've always liked San Francisco," I offered.

"Doesn't your Aunt live up there?"

"Dammit."

We batted around ideas, but I realized this was something I needed to do for and by myself.

Chem homework it was.

On the way back to my house, I considered turning the car around and driving somewhere, anywhere really.

A straight beeline to NYC or right off a cliff into the Pacific Ocean. I wasn't sure which better suited my mood.

I could get on the freeway and just drive until I ran out of gas. See where I ended up. I could go to Vegas and become a stripper. But how cliché pretty girl runaway. I could go to a Native American reservation in Oklahoma. Change my name to Eagle and grow out my hair. I could be anything but who I was, or anything but what I had become. I wanted to think, but it felt like my head had mounted itself on some malfunctioning carousel that I couldn't get off. The ride made me dizzy. Something had to give. I considered not swerving when I realized the cement island in the middle of the road was getting too close.

But I did.

I pulled into the garage and thought about how much I didn't want to go inside. I knew what was in there: chaos. No peace. No "Home Sweet Home." This is how my father must have felt, I thought, letting out an involuntary sigh. I took a deep breath and prepared myself for the act I would have to put on to conceal my depression from my mother. I wasn't sure if I could do it today, but I decided I could always pretend to be on my period, even though I hadn't seen it in months.

When I opened the front door, the house was in full swing. Three kids from down the block were shouting and running through the house as my brother, screeching at a full octave higher, chased them around the corner with a laser gun that reached a decibel I wished only dogs could hear. As far as I was concerned, whoever had bought him that gun deserved to be drawn and quartered. My Nana was cooking another boring rice-based, surely almost flavorless dinner. The TV was on. *Disney Channel*. The radio was on. *Bachata*. The dogs were barking. And my mother was trying to keep Akin and the urchins he had invited over from breaking anything in our museum-house, by shouting from the top of the stairs.

"*Hola,* Christina," I sighed, unfolding what was left of myself into a bar stool pulled up to the countertop. "*Que tal?*"

"*Ando con sueno, mi amor,*" she responded.

"*Ya lo se,*" I felt on the verge of tears suddenly.

"*Que te pasa?*" she asked, concerned enough to stop stirring some very sad-smelling sauce.

I was interrupted by my brother's bellowing "YO BIG SIS!"

"That's what the hell is wrong with me," I mumbled under my breath.

"Dootie's home!" my mother announced, descending the stairs.

I gritted my teeth, "So I am."

"How was your day?" she smiled cheerily, her neck held awkwardly due to the metal rod that was installed along her cervical spine.

I tried to swallow the angry ball in my throat. I wanted so badly to push whatever button it would take to eject that ball and direct her attention to a colorfully worded neon-sign in the living room so she could see the hurt I was bottling. Nothing else I had tried was working.

"How was my day?" I wanted to reply, sarcastically and incredulously. "My DAY?! Well, let's see... I don't know who I am anymore. I feel like I'm lost. I haven't been to English in a month. Some stupid girl in history class asked why we never talk about the benefits of slavery. Oh and to top off my ice cream cone of a day, I saw an 'I don't brake for blacks' bumper sticker on a truck on my way home. It had a little afro with skid marks through it on the side. So, if we just shelf the fact that I was raped a year ago and can't stop reliving it every single forsaken moment, how do you think today was?"

I swallowed instead. "My day was fine. I got an A on my Calculus quiz." I grinned widely for her. "How was yours?"

"Great," she said, turning away from me.

We were both lying. We were both excellent actresses. Like mother like daughter. If I remember one thing about my mother during my teen years before we lost everything, it's that no matter what happened inside the house, the second she crossed the doorframe to the outside world, she was smiling. According to our neighbors, the mailman, the grocery clerk, the gardener, my mother was always smiling. By the time we lost my childhood home, I could fake a smile better than Miss America.

I had been programmed to believe that keeping up appearances was essential to survival. Living in a volatile, explosive environment that no one knew existed formed my neuro-pathways around the following mantras: never let them see you cry. Never let anyone close enough to hurt you and thus, really know you. When the time comes that you don't really know you, smile some more.

Smiles are beautiful, but when what's behind is completely devoid of joy, they're frightening. I have a hard time looking at many of the pictures from the latter half of my childhood and teens. My eyes are more often than not disturbingly vacant. Looking at them now, it pains me to remember a time when I was so untrue to myself and my emotions that I came sprinting out of the bathroom where I had been slicing my inner thighs with a box cutter to pop my head up in the back of a group

51

picture at my little brother's twelfth birthday party. "Cheese!" And no one was any wiser. Then again neither was I. I was no wiser to the damage I was doing to myself and my ability to connect to others. I didn't want to tell anyone what had happened to me because that would make it real. Then I would have to deal with it, fix it.

And what if I couldn't?

What if I stayed broken like this forever?

The possibility that I had been permanently altered in some irreversible way was my biggest fear. I didn't want to acknowledge how I had changed. Saying I was sexually assaulted wasn't the heart of the issue. I whispered it to my mother's back every day. Told my dog every gory detail. Screamed it in the car over the wind roaring through my windows. Being sexually assaulted wasn't even the problem, per say. I didn't want to test the depth of the watery feeling that some piece of me, my innocence and ability to trust, was missing. I was afraid it lacked a sandy bottom floor. I didn't want to acknowledge the hole he had left in my chest. I figured as long as I could keep jumping over it, and keep up with my daily life, it was as if nothing had happened. But every minute I kept quiet, the hole was widening. My edges were crumbling in.

Over the course of the following year I came undone. In twenty minutes of his life, he had robbed me for the rest of mine.

I became cruel. How was I supposed to be happy now? Girls who had been finger banged against their will didn't laugh, eat ice cream sundaes or skip through daisies. They were sullen, removed. And so was I.

I tuned out the screaming kids, the blaring TV, spunky radio, and beckoned for my dog to follow me up the stairs. I tried to fight the numbness but it tingled up my legs with every step. I tried to make myself feel the carpet between my toes, my own weight sinking down onto the balls of my feet. Simple exercises like these reminded me to be present, but by the time I reached the second floor the numbness had washed over my being. I simply wasn't there anymore. Auto-pilot was on and I had no intention of turning it off. Existing in the numb space was easier than not, so I didn't fight it as much as I used to in the beginning. Turning myself off, my spirit off, my ability to feel, to care or even function was easier.

My consciousness fought desperately to burst pieces of light through the murky swamp sludge I had dove into headfirst. But the darkness closed in around my psyche as I absentmindedly turned over my Swiss Army knife in my pocket. I needed some peace, quiet and time alone with a fresh blade. We were good friends now. Me and my Swiss.

I closed the door to my bedroom and felt the adrenaline rush my brain. My forearm tingled in anticipation. Fresh cuts stung as the material of my sweater raked across sixteen deep little lines. I turned off the light switch and slid back my closet door. Behind the five by five shoe box structure I had built my safe haven, my refuge from the madness. As a little girl I had sat in the closet for hours. When my parents argued. When my brother annoyed me. When the world overwhelmed me and I simply needed to escape to my peace. When I needed to write. I cut up my Seventeen and Tiger Beat magazines and made collages on the walls. I wrote on post-its I stole from my mother's desk and covered one wall with my open conversations to God.

It was in that closet that I lost my faith.

I left my mark on the walls and carved the tragic story of my people, my sisters, into my flesh. Like a cavewoman finding artistic comfort in the dark, my hand no longer shook as I caressed my upper thigh with the blade, fishtailing it back and forth, making figure eights around a series of freckles. I fixated on one freckle and pressed the knife down harder, harder until I finally felt something. Bright red burst up around the handle. So

I dragged it. Relishing the sting, the metallic pressure, the screaming in my muscles. I controlled it all and the pain was exquisite. I wanted so desperately to feel anything, even pain, to remember that I was human. At the very least, by this physically determining factor—I was bleeding—I knew I was still alive. Because I certainly didn't feel that way anymore. I couldn't even pray.

When I wrote to Him then, I had very little to say. The post-it was the perfect sized tablet for my rage. "How could you do this to me?" "I don't know if you're real" "I'm not sure why I believe in you" "Why didn't you protect me?" "Why wasn't I worthy of your protection?" "Please help me" stacked on top of each other in the tens of hundreds. Neon yellow, green, purple. The beginnings of my atheism in day-glo. Ultimately, they were all varying messages on the same theme: abandonment. Trying to rationalize going forward with my life without God.

It didn't go over well. Post-traumatic stress disorder had a vice-tight grip on my body, soul, and mind. There was no escape option I could see from where I was sitting in the dark with my Girl Scout flashlight. I had collapsed inwards on myself and my madness exploded onto the walls. It surrounded me, swirling gently, almost erotically like a snake sensuously pulsating the life out of its prey. It closed me in until I lost all sense of who I was.

I existed in a state of agitated hypersensitivity. I had terrible nightmares and day mares. I was only safe with my eyes open and the sleep deprivation set me on edge. A slammed door or the refrigerator making ice sent me right out of my skin. The thought of anyone touching me made me simultaneously homicidal and suicidal.

I saw a few droplets of water land beside my ankle as I sat cross-legged, trying to make sense of what I was reading. Suddenly the post-its were in Japanese or hieroglyphics from some other girl's miserable, un-relatable life. When I heard my dog, Candy, whimper and scratch at the closet door only then did I realize I was crying. I think sometimes she knew before I did.

I held my legs close to my chest. I felt bones where breast tissue used to be pressed against the knobs of my knees and it dawned on me that I was dying. I slid the closet door back from inside, light flooded my eyes, and exhaustion enveloped my heart. Candy stepped half her body in the closet to rest her snout on my shoulder. She seemed tired too. She was the only being who ever dared go into that dark place with me. The only one who was brave enough to see that its uses alternated between armoire and tomb.

I wrote a note to no one in particular that began, "I wonder how long it will take you to find this." I said goodbye and requested that my babysitting money be divided amongst my three siblings. I left it on the floor of the closet. A few older post-its lost their will too and fluttered to the ground.

I pulled myself up to look in the mirror that hung on the back of my door. I didn't even know who that girl was. If I had to tell you about her I'd say she looked like an empty shell, hallowed out. Not just because anorexia and a few bulimic tendencies had taken her skin's sparkle and left her looking sallow, brittle, and breakable, but because something had happened to her.

If you had taken the time to hold her to you, you would have felt that the graveyard inside her ribcage was protruding through her sweater's best attempt to hide her upright tombstone-bones. She was grieving the death of her ability to believe in anyone or anything. And it was obvious.

There was no stability for her. She had no assurance that tomorrow wouldn't be her own personal apocalypse and she had run out of reasons to keep battling the monsters in her head. There was no point in trying to run from the numbness anymore. That soft, fuzzy, gray place depression offered so she didn't have to feel all encompassed by misery had made a ramshackle home for her now.

The drowning sensation had become ever-present. It took so much fight, too much effort just to breathe. And she was infinitely exhausted. Kicking like hell only yielded a gasp of one unfiltered breath and then she was ripped under the current again, held down by her depression right before pain becomes pleasure and everything fades white. She was dying from the inside out.

I opened the door, catching my glazed eyes in my reflection. I walked down the hall thinking these were some of my last few steps in this lifetime. I tried to imagine how an inmate who has been on death row feels when the Big Day finally comes. After all that anticipation and confinement, I wondered if any one of them felt the completely inappropriate emotions I was feeling: relief, hope, freedom.

Relief, relief, relief, I chanted to myself.

I laid down in bed letting the dizziness from a week's long hunger force me to close my eyes. I called Candy onto my bed and pulled her under the covers with me. I buried my face in the fur on her back and felt comforted knowing I wouldn't have to suffer much longer.

I was going to die tomorrow and then this would all be over.

I reached over the headboard to grab my book bag, felt around for the wider spine of my history book and pulled it in to my lap. Unhooking my flashlight from the cast iron swirls, I had already begun flipping towards the back of the book. Past the indexes and glossaries were the maps. I opened to a colorful map of the United States, closed my eyes, twirled my finger around a few times, and sung myself a little tune. I landed on Louisiana. It was bright yellow and looked a bit like a boot. I smiled at it. The capital of Baton Rouge was annotated with a purple star.

I snapped the book shut and fell asleep envisioning myself dozing off again tomorrow this time in a first class cabin on a train to Baton Rouge with the help of far too many Advil PM pills.

Hours later, I snapped awake in the middle of the night. I tried to get rid of the image of his face in my mind, but I had to catch my breath first. It was no use. That boy's face was everywhere. His ghost was haunting me and this curse possessed a much stronger juju than my fifteen years of life experience knew how to fight against. I hugged myself and tried to remember that I was safe in my bed. No one could get me. Everything was ok. The dog would bark if someone was in the house. Then his face appeared again. This time, like a monster's, laughing at me.

Candy whimpered from the foot of my bed. She had woken up and begun walking over to me slowly. She, too, had grown weary of this wretched torture. I hugged her, let out a shaky sigh then peeled the sheets off my person. The bed was soaked with sweat.

My hair was wet, my chest was slick. I called Candy down off the bed so we could cross the hall to the guest room. No way was I getting back in that bed.

Candy curled up on the right side of the bed, but positioned her head so she could keep her eye on me. She was taking the job of suicide watch very seriously. I was pleased to know that someone was paying attention.

My dad's business phone was in that room as it used to be his office and bedroom when he lived there. I picked up the phone and dialed out of the country. It took a great many digits to get to my father's cell phone but it did. It didn't ring, but instead sounded like the tone test doctors use to check your hearing as a child.

"Hello?"
A woman's voice.

"Hello?" I was startled. "Can I please speak to Akintunde?"

"Oh. Sorry. He's not here right now. May I take a message?"

I was enraged.

"Yes. Yes, you may. Please tell my father that his daughter would like to speak to him right away and as a matter of fact, if he ever wants to see me again in this life, he should come home. Immediately. It's an emergency."

"So sorry, sister. Yes of course. I will...please hold."

I figured when the number popped up on his caller ID, my dad assumed it was my mother calling with more bad news about the impending loss of our home and pawned off the call. Now that he knew it was me, he would come to the phone.

I heard some shuffling and then her sigh, "I will deliver your message."

I felt stung.

"Good. Goodbye." I slammed down the phone, tears quietly streaming down my face, and began to pack a bag.

Five

I woke up the next morning feeling as if I hadn't slept at all. I had already missed the first two periods. AP Calculus with Mr. Mansfield was third. If I could get out the door in ten minutes, I would be on time. I spent the first five minutes hugging my dog and saying goodbye to her. She sat still and heard me out.

I pulled my hair back, put on yoga pants and some strangely maroonish t-shirt my friend Sharon had made me that read "Don't hate me cuz I'm bootiful." I thought it was hilarious.

I landed in my seat exactly as the bell rang to start class. Kelly was three seats behind me and waved at me with her calculator in hand. I turned around to see that the dry erase board had the word EXAM scribbled across it in bright red. I'm not sure why but that sent me right over the edge. I burst into huge, dramatic tears.

Mr. Mansfield entered the classroom, tripped over the words, "Good morning, class!" Clearly taken aback, he caught my eye and motioned that I come with him to his office with one low, quick beckoning of his hand. I followed begrudgingly across the front of the room. All eyes on me.

He closed the office door behind us and led me to a seat by the shoulder even though I was taller than him by at least six inches.

"Shadé, are you ok?" he looked genuinely concerned.

"I'm so sorry, Mr. Mansfield. I'm so embarrassed. Please don't make me take that test today." I dissolved into tears again.

"You can take it when you're ready. Let's get you to the restroom."

"I can go by myself. Thank you, Mr. Mansfield. I really appreciate it." I wiped my face and forced a smile. It felt like my skin was cracking under the facade.

"There ya go," He smiled back at me. "That's the spirit."

I walked across his office to get to the exit that opened to main campus and gave a sheepish wave over my shoulder.

There was no one out since third period was well under way. William S. Hart High's massive campus sprawled out before me. It took me at least five minutes to reach center campus and the quad where the bathrooms were. I wasn't exactly speed walking.

There was a big brick "H" on the ground with names of big alumni donors written in black across them. I stared at the names for a while and then felt very dizzy. What was I doing out here? I got down on my hands and knees to try and steady myself. I was so lightheaded. I couldn't remember the last time I had eaten anything at all. And kept it down. I unfolded myself out across the H and tried to get my limbs as far apart from each other as I could.

I wonder how long I've been here, I thought suddenly. Any minute now 4,000 of my peers could come barreling out of those doors and I would be unable to get myself upright. Losing my cool status was certainly not a major threat but still, I had shame.

I turned over on to my belly and saw the bathroom swirling up ahead. No more than twenty yards, I thought. I crawled across the asphalt, scraping my hands and knees. I'm sure one of the

60

security guards saw me, but I had mouthed off to them too many times about my illegal parking in the teacher's lot and how an ID card system was futile unless it was electronic. Truth was, I couldn't wake up early enough to get to the student lot before it was full and I couldn't remember to bring my ID card to school half the time. Having some 40 year old woman with a bad perm, weirdly hot pink glitter lip gloss, and a whistle around her neck yell at me about how "the rules applied to everyone" was not what I needed.

So I made it to the bathroom unseen by anyone who cared and pulled myself up by the sink. Kelly appeared just then.

"I finished my test as fast as I could," she reported and ran into one of the bathroom stalls.

She promptly stood on the toilet and announced, "Come here."

"What are you doing?" I asked totally bewildered.

"The best hugs come from people who are taller than you and you probably don't get those that often. So..." She motioned for me to enter the stall.

I obliged.

She hugged me back and she was right; it was the best hug.

"Ok, let's go," I sniffed and collected myself.

"Go?"

"Yes. Go."

"Ok," she smiled as if she suddenly remembered a beach trip we had been planning and scooped up her book bag on the way out the door. Odd, I thought. But Kelly was odd. It was one of the best things about her.

We climbed into my car and even though no one was allowed to leave the lot until lunch period I knew I could get away with it somehow.

Sure enough we sailed right past the security guard and turned onto Lyon's Avenue.

Kelly didn't ask where we were going and I loved her for it.

We bumped over the railroad tracks, and I slowed down as the Old Newhall train station came into view.

"What the hell, Shadé?" she finally blurt out.

I parked the car, popped the trunk, and hopped out in nearly one motion. I felt energized for the first time in what seemed like years.

"Shadé!"

I ignored her, grabbed my backpack, and double checked the folder for my report cards, social security card, birth certificate, and immunization records. Envelope of money? Check.

"Shadé!" her voice was breaking now.

"I'll be fine, Kelly. Can you please be strong?"

"Where are you going?!"

"I'm getting on this train," I answered her methodically. "It'll be here in two minutes. You can take the car."

I tossed her the keys and she caught them as if they weighed thirty pounds.

"What?!" she was horrified and openly crying now.

I boarded the train and waved to her out the window. She didn't wave back. She held my gaze and cried. Her mouth was open and she looked so confused. The train seemed to take forever to leave the station. I turned away first because I couldn't explain. Not from my window seat anyway.

I think that's why I thought suicide or running away were my best options. I didn't know how to explain myself. What happened to me? What had become of me? I didn't know either.

The train arrived in Los Angeles, blocks from the infamous Skid Row and the outdoor shopping carts and snacks that made Olvera Street such a blast. I had come there years ago with my Girl Scout troop when we were learning about the history of Los Angeles and studying the missions. A bird had pooped on my troop leader's head and I nearly keeled over laughing.

I walked into the station. It was filled with old art deco charm and the high ceilings were so romantic. I stood in the very long line and watched the cities and arrival times continuously adjust. I hadn't even looked at them to know when the train was leaving to Baton Rouge.

"Next!"

I shuffled over to the teller, unprepared.

"Hi, umm. One ticket to Baton Rouge please."

"Round trip?"

"No, just one way. Thanks."

"ID please," she said suspiciously.

"Oh, sure," I fumbled, certain I had already made a mistake.

"That train doesn't leave for another three hours. And you'll have to stop in Chicago first."

I felt like she slapped me. Three hours. Kelly was already home. She had already told her mom. Who had already called my mom. Who had already called the police. I had to get out of here. Now, not three hours from now.

I kicked myself for not checking the departures times earlier. Why did I say Baton Rouge? Could I change my answer? Was it too late?

I felt resigned. There was no way I was going back to that house. I paid for the ticket in cash and walked back out on to the streets of LA. To either kill some time or kill myself. I wasn't sure which yet.

I strolled down Olvera Street and bought a huge burrito that was made on top of a push cart by a small woman wearing a 1980s looking Luther Vandross t-shirt. It was delicious. I walked down to see what the other carts had to offer and stopped one that was covered in funky, little handmade hats. I had always like hats.

I picked out a blue one with a little rolled rim. I looked at myself in the hand mirror a very tiny, rude woman thrust into my face with an annoyed grunt. "You'd think you didn't want to sell any hats," I mumbled.

"Haaah?" she inquired in a thick accent, shaking the mirror slightly to insinuate that she wasn't going to hold it for me any longer. I gingerly took it from her, catching a glimpse of my protruding cheekbones in my reflection. I couldn't remember the last time I looked myself in the eye in a mirror. I was considering the probability that it would end badly when I heard her squawk, "You buy something?" I glanced at her sour face out of the corner of my eye. She was about six inches away from me. Did she really think I was gonna steal one of her tacky hats? I gave her the five dollars she barked at me for in a wadded ball on general principle.

I asked someone for the time and realized I had only killed twenty minutes. I thought it had been at least an hour. There was no way I was gonna make it three hours. So my exit wouldn't be as graceful as the first class cabin final nap I had envisioned. I had forgotten to ask for the cabin price and reservation anyway. There went that.

Improvise, improvise, I thought to myself, and took a breath I tried not to exhale as a defeated sigh.

I closed my eyes and listened to the people, sounds, and cars around me. LA is never one to allow such romance so I opened my eyes when a homeless woman who was strung out on something vicious touched my arm. I realized she was trying to take what was left of my burrito out of my hand, but was none too slick. I handed it to her. She smiled at me softly and I could tell that she might have once been very beautiful underneath the veil drugs had cast over her face.

I kept walking. I had no idea where I was going, but things got quieter and quieter after just a few minutes trek. I looked around to see a bunch of old trains and at least five sets of tracks lined up across the street. There were no cars on the road so I strode across and threw my backpack over the fence. The barbed wire had already been snipped in that spot by someone whose intentions were probably much different from mine.

I took in the scenery. Wasn't much to look at. Dirty, grimy, industrial. A far cry from plush velvet seats and the hope of a cute waiter who'd serve an underage girl her first and last glass of wine.

I sat down on the middle track and looked up at the sky. I'm not really certain why I got naked. Maybe I just wanted to go out the way I came in. I undressed and folded my clothes into a pillow. I laid down on the tracks. They were scorching hot.

65

I gritted my teeth and started talking aloud to God. I told him every lie I ever told, every person I ever hurt. I confessed it all. Most of what I considered to be sins were my feelings. The repulsion I felt for my brother's touch; my frustration at my mother's obliviousness; the anger I felt towards my father which was applicable to all men nowadays.

So I laid there and God and I had it out.

Six

When asked why it took me so long to tell anyone what happened, I didn't really have an answer then. But I do now. I didn't feel like I had a strong enough family support system. My father was gone and my mother was newly disabled, so very sad and well-aware that we were headed for bankruptcy. I was guilt-ridden at the mere thought of burdening her further. I wanted to be perfect for her and I no longer felt like a child in her eyes. I spent months convincing myself that what happened in the closet wasn't a big deal. I was fine. He didn't have sex with me. I just had to stay busy. It wasn't a big deal. It wasn't a big deal. It wasn't a big deal.

I think I wanted someone else to start a conversation with me or to have some sort of lead in. I was an awkward fifteen year old with a frizzy fro and terrible taste in eyeliner. What was I supposed to do? Pull aside my favorite English teacher and say, "Hey, Mrs. Ladd. Oh no, I'm doing fine with *The Grapes of Wrath*. I was wondering if we could talk about... um. This is weird for me. So last fall..."

College campuses seem far more willing to discuss rape, put up rape crisis phone numbers in the student center, and advertise PSAs on their radio or local stations. Why aren't high schools doing the same?

We had speakers come to preach the dangers of drunk driving and drug use, the importance of academic integrity. I personally knew of three girls and one boy in my grade alone who needed another speaker far more: a compassionate voice against violence to let us know that no one had the right to make us feel unsafe, hurt us, or force us to do anything we didn't want to do. We needed to know that the forgetfulness, slipping grades, self-hatred, promiscuity and exhaustion wasn't our fault. But no such voice ever came.

There was one sliver of hope in the year I kept quiet.

"Tomorrow, instead of bio lab, we're going to have a speaker. She's going to talk to you guys about sex and STDs."

As soon as I saw her I knew more harm than good would be done. Glaring at us through her horn-rimmed glasses and shaking her gray-streaked mullet off her shoulders in sharp, sudden, tick-like movements, she told our class a story about how her prehistoric abortion had robbed her of the ability to have children forever and if she hadn't been such a slutty, slutty teenager, such an atrocity would have never happened.

"I regret that I ever had sex," she reported, not with lament or earnest despair, but with an alarming bite.

"It cost me the future I always dreamed of having. It was the biggest mistake of my entire life."

I saw her eyes dart at the cleavage my tank top was showing off and look away in disapproval. She announced we weren't allowed to leave the room until we signed a contract, vowing not to have sex until we were adults. My eyebrows were raised into my hairline and my chin found a comfortable resting place on my desk for most of her speech. God forgive me, but the thought that perhaps this woman wasn't meant to be a mother definitely crossed my mind. Scared or shamed straight, the rest of the class swarmed the front of the room while I snuck out the back exit.

Since our school lacked funding for proper sexual education, that was it. Either that or the uber-conservative agenda had prevailed again.

I actually didn't tell my mother I had been sexually assaulted. She guessed. The day the police found me at Union Station with a one-way ticket to Baton Rouge in my pocket and my signature curls tucked into that hideous blue hat, my mother said, "Ok, you have my attention."

And I realized that was all I had really wanted.

Now that I had it, ironically enough, I was completely speechless. She began tentatively trying options for why this skeletal girl of hers was sitting next to her with all she deemed worthy of necessary to start a new life in a backpack in the trunk.

It was surreal.

I don't really remember if we spoke on the way back to the house.

I was barely there at all.

When we got back to the house, no one was around. I don't know where Akin was, but the house was quiet. Our house was never quiet.

My mom and I walked up the staircase to her office. I dragged my feet meaningfully over the top and round of each step. I had lost.

I wasn't really certain if I was going to be punished or if she was feeling compassionate towards what was left of me or if she was going to call my dad and make him deal with me. I felt completely at her mercy. I didn't particularly want to explain what my plan had been or why I had chosen Baton Rouge specifically or what had happened on the train tracks to make me limp up the stairs. I felt like an open wound. No guards up.

No fight left. She sat at her desk chair and swiveled out to face me.

My father's desk on the opposite side of the office, empty of him for months yet covered in papers, pictures, and receipts as if he were there yesterday.

I sat, for symbolic reasons, in between their two desks, on the ground. Not at his desk as I had for so many conversations between my mother and I. I could no longer sit in his place. It was killing me and ruining our relationship.

I studied the fibers of the carpet. Dirt, dog hair, dust, potato chip fragment.

"Shadé."

She sounded far away.

"Yes."

"What is going on with you?"

I sighed and shook my head.

"Do you miss your Daddy?"

I shook my head.

"Are you unhappy at your new school?"

I shook my head.

"Did something happen?"

I stiffened. She thought for a moment in silence and tentatively tried again.

"Did someone touch you?"

I felt her words break through the rubber inner tube that was surrounding my psyche. It was excruciating.

I looked up from the dust and dog hair only to collapse further to the floor than I already was.

I used the last ounce of strength I had to tell her what happened. I don't remember what degree of detail I told her or what exactly I said.

I only remember how I began.

"It was last year. And I didn't know how to tell you because I thought I could deal with it by myself. You have enough on your plate with Akin and Dad and I didn't want to be another burden."

She cried.

I was relieved. At least she wasn't mad. I crawled over to her and laid my head in her lap.

I had just transferred to Chaminade College Preparatory, a fancy schmancy private school in Woodland Hills. I wanted to go to Mt. St. Mary's, an all girls' school in Beverly Hills, but the commute was too intense even without factoring in West LA traffic.

Chaminade had all the main bells and whistles I was looking for. A challenging curriculum, small class sizes, college bound students, and some diversity worth mentioning. I could get over the fact that it was co-ed. Even at fourteen years old, I was largely uninterested in boys. I had one crush, Frankie, in eighth grade. He came up to my shoulder and we only flirted on occasion when no one was looking.

Leaving him behind was no major loss. I could maintain my girl friendships with Kelly and Kristin. No problem.

So after one torturous, under stimulated year spent in public school I trotted off to find that indeed the grass was greener on the other side.

No one was tongue kissing ferociously in the hall; no scent of marijuana was wafting into the science lab from the baseball field; the track was Olympic standard; no one stared at me like I was an alien because I wasn't white or Mexican or Asian; none of the girls took pride in being a skateboarding, bleached blonde, beauty school drop out; no condoms were inflated at the pep rallies; no teachers began their introductions to their classes with "I don't want to be here anymore than you do." My nerd-heart was overjoyed.

Social skills weren't my forte because I was so different as a child. I've never made friends easily. Trust is hard-won from me, and I take my time to get to know someone and feel comfortable enough to be myself. For years, I might present "Showtime Shadé," unless some catastrophe forces me to stop production.

At Chaminade, I made friends with the dorky girls. They were more my speed anyway. Finding a tight-fitting polo shirt, getting fake nails, a fake tan, a dog-tag necklace from Tiffany's and a pair of expensive boat shoes were not on my to-do list. So off to my fellow friendly and zitty-nosed comrades for lunch it was.

We were one month into the school year and I was happy with my niche. I hopped around campus and said hi to others but my friend base was sturdy.

I made my loyalties known and was surprised to receive an invitation to a birthday party from two boys in my grade. I had hardly spoken to any boys at all.

I pretended to have a boyfriend who went to my "old school" but refused to provide many further details.

Wow, I thought, feeling the computer printout paper grain in my fingers.

I stuffed it in my bag quickly. A pretty sandy blonde haired girl named Kevyn smiled at me and told me I was invited to her boyfriend's joint birthday party with his best friend, Robert. They were both tall, smart, goofy, and athletic. To be honest, I wasn't sure why I was being invited. Just in case my friends weren't, I planned not to bring it up. I felt bewildered.

Was I supposed to tell them I got an invitation? Would they feel betrayed if they found out I had gone to the party behind their backs?

Thank God. The entire tenth grade was invited. Liz, Rachel, Marianne, and Monica scoffed at their invitations. Not interested. Parents would never agree. I'd only go if you were going.

"I think I want to go," I offered quietly.

And thus was the beginning of the end of our friendship.

I became slightly obsessed with the party. I had never been invited to such an event before. A huge mansion in the hills. A sound system that blasted music through every room in the house. Basketball and tennis courts. Two pools.

Stars in my eyes, I shopped for different parts of my outfit every day after school. Shoes, jewelry, hair accessories. I tried different hair styles. The end result was a hot pink v-necked tank top, jeans that had pink stitching and matching butterfly decals on the butt, silver sandals, a crucifix my sister had given me, and silver hoop earrings I found at Clarie's for a dollar. I must have looked like a disaster, but I loved it then.

Finally the night came and I had made better friends with a few girls I knew were going to the party. Lily in particular. She told crass jokes and had tried every drug there was, but she was free-spirited and accepting. She always seemed to smile genuinely when I talked to her.

I was on the younger side of 15 and not old enough to get my permit yet. My mom's assistant, Claudia, picked me up from school and drove me to things like lessons, friend's houses, and basketball practices. Thus she was called on to take me to and from Ryan and Robert's Sweet 16.

I dressed myself painstakingly. Shaved every inch of myself that I could reach. Arms, stomach, toes. I put the blow-dryer on a low setting so the heat wouldn't damage my curls and just sat there staring at myself, listening to music for hours, putting on makeup, taking it off, trying again.

I was so excited I couldn't keep my hand still enough to apply my glittery purple eyeliner. (P.S. whoever invented glittery purple eyeliner is cruel. You knew teens would buy it hoping to distract from their orthodontia challenges and look like rejects from a pop music video audition in the process. But you did it anyway. Shame on you.)

I filled a small silver purse with lip gloss, my Chaminade ID card, my cell phone, and $20 just in case.

I announced myself ready to Claudia who was waiting for me on the living room couch.

"Bye, Mom!" I called up the stairs to her. She was at her desk. I heard her ancient chair squeal and whine as she turned to direct her voice back down to me. "Have fun! Call Claudia an hour before you're ready to come home!"

"Got it!" Something about that house required you to be a shouter.

Anyway, off Claudia and I went. Windows down, music blaring, we car danced and laughed the whole hour and a half drive there. Claudia brought out the free spirit in me.

She told me to have a great time as I skipped out of the car. I had to remind myself to walk calmly up the stately, shrub-lined walkway to their doorstep.

It was Ryan's parents' home. They opened the massive door, greeted me, and offered me a Sprite.

Music was playing and my classmates were dashing all over the estate. Up and down stairs. Laughing. Jumping into the pool. Big smiles.

I pulled out my phone to text Lily that I had arrived, but she smacked me on the arm first.

"Hey girl! You made it," she whipped her long hair over her shoulder.

"Yup!" I chirped back.

"Wanna see the house?" she said with a mischievous glint in her eye.

"Yeah!" I offered some enthusiasm.

We wandered around the estate, stopping to talk, laugh, dance in pre-formed groups. I took in the abundant wealth, over the top gadgets, and the elegant grace of Ryan's mother.

I was in awe for at least the first hour. But I relaxed eventually and went off exploring on my own.

Each room was different, full of different people, containing its own energy.

One group was playing truth or dare.

One was just full of kids kissing.

I slammed the door, nervous and horrified.

I still hadn't kissed anyone yet.

It was sacred to me. I certainly didn't want to witness some slobbery teenage disaster that involved the swapping of Winterfresh gum.

I remember thinking I felt like Alice in Wonderland, "I wonder what's behind this door." I finally found a room and mood that suited me. People were just sitting down on the floor, talking, telling stories.

"What's the grossest thing that's ever happened to you?"

I sat down in the corner furthest away from the current storyteller so I would have plenty of time to perfect my tale, and figure out where the best opportunities for jokes and sarcasm were.

I faded in and out of the conversation so I could get a good gauge on how much planning time I had left; there was something about a very broken arm on a bike ride, a mishap with a zipper, a babysitting disaster, and then it was my turn.

It's the one detail of the night I don't remember. I was so fixated on whether or not my peers would like me that the only memories I have of my story telling session are their faces, their expectant smiles, laughter, hoots, and my feeling of relief and acceptance.

I sat in the awkwardly shaped circle in my bliss as the group grew and the story telling was forgotten.

I slunk into the corner to text Claudia that I would like to go home soon.

I was sitting next to the opening of a huge walk-in closet and before I could unzip my purse I was shoved backwards inside the closet.

I rolled over backwards twice like I had a thousand times in tumbling class before the coach pulled my mother's assistant aside to tell her that I would definitely be too tall to ever be a gymnast.

I stood up, annoyed, assuming it was an accident and that someone would rush in any moment, full of apologies.

But it took too long.

My head spun. Something wasn't right.

And then the light was blocked out.

A shadow of a boy.

In Search of My Father

Seven

He was tall with broad shoulders. A football player's build.

I didn't recognize him, but I felt the energy of his intention course up and down the walls of the small space we were in.

Get out; get out; get out, every cell in my body screamed. My brain told my feet to do all the right things, but they were glued to the ground.

I was terrified. Not necessarily because of him, but because I had already given up. He hadn't touched me or even said anything and I had already decided he was in control.

He lumbered towards me and it seemed suddenly he was on top of me.

To say that I remember every detail of being sexually assaulted would be an outright lie. Psychologically, the amount of work I have done to block the event could parallel chain gang ditch digging daily for a year straight.

My memories of being in that closet come back to me out of order, in strange swatches: most of them are murky, dark and distorted; some are bright, brilliant flashes of red violating pain, and the rest are dark blue with devastation.

I can recall one quick flash of him on top of me, but interestingly enough most of my memories are of his back. As if I was somehow on the ceiling, looking down at myself, observing powerlessly. As if I was watching a movie and had no way to pause, rewind, eject. I see my own face, my own eyes brimming with horror, then eerily vacant.

I remember the way he smelled. More than I remember anything else. The scent of his cologne, I will never forget. To this day I avoid men's cologne counters in department stores because I don't want to put a name to his scent. I once left in the middle of a first date. He was wearing it. Luckily, the scent has either lost popularity or been discontinued.

I remember that his hands were rough, like he was an athlete or spent time weightlifting. His fingertips were like sand paper against the skin under my shirt.

I remember that he pressed on me, my hips, my ribs. It felt like he was purposefully pushing harder than necessary to lift himself up, like he was reminding me that he was stronger.

I remember that he fumbled with the button on my pants. He had given up on his own jeans and apparently too complicated belt.

I remember that he seemed out of it. Not really drunk, but that he moved slowly, awkwardly, like his fingers had minimal dexterity. Maybe he was on drugs. He drooled on me as he grunted in my ear. Repulsion skated over my skin. Like water moving over the scales of a reptile, I absorbed the chilly fear despite the best efforts nature had afforded me to harden myself. I held every muscle I could control as tightly as possible, clenched my fists. I closed my eyes and went as far away from that closet as I could.

I remember crying quietly as he jammed his fingers inside me over and over and over again. It felt like ripping, tearing, scratching. It was the most outrageous pain I had ever felt. I had never even used a tampon. He brought his face down to mine

80

and I turned away. When he buried his face in my neck, I was relieved. I didn't want my first kiss to be with a rapist. My ears filled with my tears, manipulating the sounds he made to give them a muffled, whale-like quality.

I remember that he was very heavy. He was crushing my crucifix into my sternum.

He lifted himself up to try and get his pants off again, but I couldn't stand the thought of having sex with him. So I kicked him as hard as I could. I gave it all I had. He fell over backwards with a thud, hitting his head on the floor. I noticed his hair was blonde as I dashed past him to the sliding door. I ripped it wide open. I felt a flush as the air hit my face and the realization that at least fifteen people had heard me crying, whimpering, begging for help washed over me. And no one had come for me.

Through the blur of my tears I saw their expressions: smirks, disgust, shock. I opened my mouth to defend myself, to say something, but I followed their eyes to my unbuttoned pants. Shame and embarrassment flooded my being. They assumed I had wanted it. When all I wanted now was to die. Gossiping whispers followed me as I limped softly to the bathroom down the hall.

I closed the bathroom door behind me and put my purse on the counter. I had to urinate but I knew it would hurt so I decided to hold it. I placed my hands on the counter, daring myself to look at my reflection.

"Look up, look up, look up," I said just loud enough for myself to hear.

It sounded like someone else's voice.

There was still water in my ears.

I couldn't look at myself. I stared at my toes instead. They were

81

hot pink.

My hands started sweating on the tile and slipping even though I tried to grip the ridge.

"Hello?" Someone knocked on the door.

"Someone's in here!" I snarled, meaner than I had intended.

"Gosh," she sounded like Sarah in my biology class. She had been my lab partner once. I immediately felt a pang of guilt.

"Bitch," she whispered through the crack in the door, and my guilt was instantly erased.

I spoke to myself out loud again. "Ok, Shadé. You can do this. Ready? One, two, three."

I flashed my eyes up quickly and held my own gaze.

It was true.

"No, no, no, no, no, no, no, no, no," I sobbed and let myself fold into a trembling heap on the floor.

I think I had been hoping it hadn't happened, that maybe it really had been a movie or that I had finally completely lost my mind and hallucinated the whole thing.

But I knew staring at my reflection that it was too true. I balled up the bath mat in my arms and yanked it tightly to my chest.

"You've got to toughen up, Shadé," I growled at the terry cloth in my hands.

"Get tough!" I was practically shouting now, gripping that stupid mat like I wished I had the back of that guy's head.

I stood up, washed my face and scrubbed it as hard as I could, wiped it on a hand towel that probably cost more than my whole outfit put together and then I called Claudia to come pick me up.

I resolved not to tell a soul. I would take this to my grave. I held my head high and I opened the door to a full line of antsy girls along the wall. "Aren't there, like, a million other bathrooms?" I muttered as I walked by, avoiding their stares. There was a huge water splash right down the center of my top. I had taken off all my makeup and pulled my hair into a bun. Their eyes followed after me as I marched down the stairs.

When I got outside, I saw Claudia waiting for me.

Thank God, I mumbled.

She honked the horn and I all but flew out of my skin. The hyper vigilance had already begun. I don't really remember what Claudia and I talked about in the car. I assume she asked me about the party and I gave her empty answers. I wanted to get home and shower. Desperately.

When we parked in the garage, I didn't wait for her to get out too like I usually did. "Thanks, Claudia," I called over my shoulder and dashed up the stairs.

"Hi, Mom," I whispered loudly in the direction of her office and tucked into the bathroom across the hall. I immediately began running the water.

"Hey, Noon," she said through the door. "How was the party? Did you have a good time?"

"Great! Super fun!" I smiled hard. "Gonna shower!"

"Ok, glad you had fun," she said. "Come say good night when you're done."

I clenched my fists.

I climbed into the tub with my clothes on and let the shower run over me. I laid there for a while and tried to stop the flashes of being in the closet from running through my head.

After struggling to get my tight and now sopping wet jeans off, I decided to get out of the shower and grab the medical scissors out of the cabinet. I cut the tank top down the center though I probably could have gotten it off on my own. I sliced two long cuts down the front of both the pant legs and peeled off my jeans. I left the scissors on the counter and got back into the shower.

I picked up my loofah, covered it in soap and started scrubbing. I scrubbed and scrubbed and scrubbed. All over, every painstaking inch. The blood in my underwear had surprised me when they fell to my ankles. I knew it wasn't my period and felt so ashamed. I berated myself for not fighting back sooner. Why hadn't I protected myself? Why did I just lay there? I scrubbed harder. Why didn't I yell or scream as loud as I could right in his ear? I scrubbed myself raw.

When I got out of the shower, the bathroom was completely full of steam. I wiped a clearing in the mirror but didn't dare to look myself in the eye again. I saw the scissors out of the corner of my eye and picked them up by the handle like a dagger.

I wrapped the towel around myself and spun my hair into a bun. I held my left arm out and made a fist as if I was preparing to give blood. Well, I suppose I was.

I raked the scissors across my forearm over and over again. The lines were small and the blood appeared slowly in misaligned droplet formations. I tilted my arm down and watched the blood trickle down to my wrist.

"Noon! Time for bed" my mother called from her office.

84

I was so startled I dropped the scissors and knocked over a few plastic cups into the sink. They made hallow clanging noises against each other until they cluttered to a stop.

"Whoa," I whispered under my breath.

That was the first time I had ever cut myself. And I liked it.

I stayed in that creepy, self-destructive, half-insane, self-loathing space for a year. It was a year of excruciating silence. Every day I kept quiet, I fed my rage and the power of PTSD. Three hundred and sixty five days marked by piping hot showers, three, sometimes as many as six times a day. I would pumice, scrape, scratch, and sit and scrub until the skin of this whore he had made me become, came off.

I hated myself.

From the night of the rape to the day I ran away, the intensity only escalated. Someone touched my arm at school. The spot they had touched would pulsate, tingle and almost throb with the filth they had left behind. I'd have to ditch the rest of the day so I could shower. I smelled someone's cologne at the mall; shower. I had a flashback; shower. I felt scared watching some variation on a cops and robbers TV show; shower, shower, shower.

As drained as I was throughout the day, I always had enough energy left to hate myself. I remember being so exhausted after those showers. The steam made it difficult to breathe without getting lightheaded and I could never scrub quite hard enough. It seems I was in that shower for a year, wearing away under the force of my own hand. The first time I didn't cut myself or try to scrub to the point of pain was in the shower after I came home from the train station.

After I talked, I was free. When the silence was broken so was the curse. I knew when I emerged the truth was waiting for me out there. It felt so liberating. The truth was cleaner than I could ever get myself with all the tools Bed, Bath, and Beyond could afford me. I thought the lie would be easier, but I couldn't have been more wrong. Lying to myself and withholding that truth from those who loved me almost cost me my life.

So instead of doing my usual post-shower thirty minute cutting routine and crying session over how I couldn't focus in school and hated everyone, this time, I toweled off and packed up bags. I didn't even notice that I had cruised right passed the medical scissors; I was too excited and anxious about moving in with my Aunt Virginia and Uncle Darrell.

Eight

A little over a week had passed since my attempt to run away from home and/or kill myself failed. My Aunt Virginia and my mom were sitting in the living room discussing a place a few blocks away from my aunt's house called the Rape Treatment Center of Santa Monica. It was a branch of UCLA.

I eavesdropped for a while at first, but it all seemed like things I could hear so I decided to reveal myself from behind the wall that angled into the kitchen.

"Hey," I mumbled awkwardly.

"Hi, Shadé," my aunt said gently. I could tell she had been crying.

I felt so uncomfortable in my own skin and I was so bony I could hardly sit on anything other than three stacked pillows and feel remotely alright. I tried to hold eye contact with my aunt but I couldn't. She had one of those gazes that forced you to tell the truth and I really didn't want to yet. I had been lying for so long; it was my comfort zone now.

I listened while she told me about the success stories of the Rape Treatment Center, how they were trained to work especially with rape survivors, and that her son's bedroom was mine as long as I wanted it. He had gone off to college the year before.

I took in all the information and was quite frankly overwhelmed. Was she an angel? She had just flown in here and commanded the whole situation and it seemed instantly everything was going to be alright. When a mere week ago, everything was so clearly going to be over.

In the seven day interim, my mother sent me to a child and family therapist who worked near our local hospital, Henry Mayo Memorial. His name sounded a lot like Fuzzy Bastard. Obviously, I'm in no position to make fun of anyone's name regarding ease of pronunciation. Au contraire, Dr. Bastard earned his nickname with me for his starring role in a forty minute interrogation guised as a therapy session so offensive I had to walk out ten minutes early.

As stranger rapes are rare, he told me he didn't think my "story" made sense and asked me the same questions repeatedly, in random order so he could try to catch me in a lie.

He had a list of facts on clipboard that he kept referencing like it was my rap sheet.

"I see here that you bought a train ticket to Baton Rouge," he glanced up over his glasses. There was no fleck of compassion in his eyes. "Why did you choose that city?"

"Umm, it was random. I don't know."

"How did you afford that ticket?"

"I had my babysitting money saved up. I had been thinking about running away for over a year."

"Have you ever stolen from your mother before?"

"A few bucks for ice cream when I was a little girl, but I wouldn't really call that stealing from my mother."

"Why did you choose that particular day to run away from home?"

"No special reason for that day," I tried to think, but I could feel him staring at me. "I don't know."

"You don't know?"

I couldn't stop fidgeting. Tears welled in my eyes.

"Why are you mad at me?" I mumbled under my breath.

"What was that?" he replied sharply, clicking his pen to the ready position to write down whatever it was I had said.

Apparently, that was the only thing I said worth writing down.

"Nothing," I sighed and looked up at the clock. This was going to be a long fifty minutes.

Had he dimmed a flickering light, turned up the heat, and gruffly shoved me into a metal chair with a wobbly leg, I would have been better prepared for his rapid fire questioning and attempts to condemn me as a lying whore.

He pressed on "I'm finding it hard to believe you don't know anyone in Baton Rouge. Did you meet someone online that you wanted to meet in person? Was it frightening when the police apprehended you at the train station? Did you feel like you needed to just say something so your mom wouldn't be mad at you? I heard you were unhappy with your high school."

I hadn't spoken in a solid five minutes.

I have never been so insulted by anyone in my entire life; did he seriously just insinuate that I had been en route to consummate my virtual love for some perverted serial killer with a receding hairline on Myspace who was using a Backstreet Boys's blurry black and white headshot as his profile pic? And that said perv-killer actually convinced the honor roll student to throw it all away and get on a two day long train ride headed for a small town surrounded by alligator-infested swamps, rife for the dumping of bodies? Yes, an internet boyfriend was his theory and he was convinced it was fact. I sat stunned as he continued.

"I've heard this story before," his eyes sparkled with the accusations he wanted to hurl at me. Tears streamed down my face, as the rest of his theory unfolded. "Young girls get scared when they get caught and they feel embarrassed."

"But that's not what happened," I said in a small voice.

"Oh, ok," he said full of exaggerated interest. "Why don't you tell me what really happened?"

I didn't see the point. He had already made up his mind about me and teenage girl runaways. Obviously, when I got caught trying to make a break for the arms of my backwoods beloved, I just stumbled upon the idea of making up a rape and resulting psychological disorder, so that I could achieve my truer, alternative goal: dropping out of high school. These were worse than fighting words in my book. This was an obscene, slanderous insult to an injury he couldn't even begin to comprehend.

I wasn't a deceitful dingbat moonlighting as a pedophile's obsession, putting on webcam shows using my mom's Compaq desktop. And I most certainly was not looking for an excuse to be lazy. I resented his egregious allegations and I let him know it. How dare he condemn me? When I packed a bag to start my new life in Baton Rouge, I brought my report cards so that I could go back to school; not a box of condoms so I could boink my new boyfriend. It was over ten years ago that I met Dr. Bastard and my skin still prickles with the rage I felt that day.

I was a broken girl who needed help, not judgmental needling and heartless, baseless accusations. I hated that bastard and refused to ever go back.

This was my first experience with therapy. My first experience telling someone outside my family that I had been hurt. I still had rows of fresh cuts on my forearms I had carved there mere days ago and I needed to talk about the failing grades, the disinterest in sports, friends, parties, books, my body, myself, my life. I wanted to say, someone took that from me and I need help getting it back. Dr. Bastard took the honor of that disclosure from me.

I slammed the door to his office when I stormed out, relishing the sound of a picture frame that must have been hanging on the wall, crashing to the ground. I remember hoping it was his diploma shattering into a thousand pieces so that my exit would have symbolically implicated how little he deserved to practice therapy.

I hope he comes across this book one day and knows how much I wish I could take that license away from him. I was a child who walked into his office seeking refuge and he might as well have slapped me across the face. The best I can do now is pray to God that no child who has been sexually assaulted ever again cross his doorframe. Because they will find no solace on the other side.

It had never occurred to me, after all this time in silence, that someone wouldn't believe me when I finally decided to speak up. I could scarcely muster the courage to tell my mother what had happened. She looked so hopeful, so anxious when I came home.

"How did it go?" she asked as I closed the front door behind me. Her eyes were bloodshot and exhausted.

I told her the truth anyway.

I hadn't realized how much it meant to me that she believed me until that moment. She didn't ask for proof or if I had been drinking or if I was flirting with him. She didn't insinuate that I somehow brought the rape on myself with my hot pink outfit. She didn't ask me not to tell people because she was ashamed of me too. And I'm so grateful. Because the very thought of her saying any one of those things to me feels like a knife in the heart.

I didn't know how important it was that I utilize rape-sensitive resources. Recovering from a rape isn't like getting over divorce, or financial ruin, or really like anything else at all. Friends, parents, teachers, spouses are truly ill-equipped to give the kind of support it takes to heal. Not for any shortcomings of their own but simply because this type of trauma can create one of the most complex psychological disorders categorized: post traumatic stress disorder.

I don't think people understand what rape is or what it does to a psyche. I don't think people understand the gravity of what they are asking a survivor to overcome when they require immediate healing, denial or composure. Or, at least I hope not. Too often rape survivors are bullied during their attempts to report a rape to police, accused of being too flirtatious, too promiscuous by friends or perhaps worst of all, forced to keep vile and disgusting family secrets. There is no security in a lie. A quote by Buddha sums up my thoughts regarding this subject quite well, "Three things cannot be long hidden: the sun, the moon, and the truth."

It is my current opinion that professional specialized psychological help is imperative. Unfortunately, at sixteen years old, I had no idea what I was supposed to do to "get better." I was at the mercy of my parents and their ideas. After that miserable failure in therapy, my father suggested I go to Nigeria with him and attend a very prestigious all-girls school. If only the very thought of studying for their entrance exam didn't make me want to find another set of train tracks. I knew I wanted my dad. If he would come home, I stood a chance. So I took to begging.

I was on the phone with him in the kitchen, sobbing.

"Daddy, I'm not ok!" I nervously twirled one sad curl around my finger until it broke off, brittle and ruined into the palm of my hand.

I paced the tile and threw the curl in the trashcan, making sure to push it to the bottom so no one would be alarmed.

I carried on, "I can't sleep because I keep having nightmares. I'm not hungry and when I force myself it makes me feel so sick. I've been throwing up for a long time now." I tried not to bite my thin nails. I was dizzy as usual so I tried to steady myself by balancing my elbows on the edge of the sink. It was awkward and it hurt. Suddenly, I was completely overwhelmed, "I'm dying, Daddy. And I'm going to die if you don't come home." I looked around me, trying to make my eyes focus.

"I hate it here so much! I just want my Daddy back." He hadn't spoken a single word. The silence was more than I could stomach. I held the phone away from my mouth and vomited into the kitchen sink. Everything was so awkward. Everything was so painful.

Finally, I just exploded, "Daddy! Please! Please! Just come home for a little while. Please!"

I was shaking as I hung my head. I was too exhausted to hold it up anymore and I already knew what he would say.

He took a deep breath and sighed, "Ashani, I can't..."

I struggled to draw in a ragged breath. It seemed like all the air had been sucked out of the room. I felt like a fish out of water, watching the kitchen swim around me as the refrigerator, oven and dishwasher's shape became distorted beyond recognition.

He was mid-sentence and I heard his garbled voice reaching up to me as the phone fell from the cradle I had made for it on my shoulder and clamored into the kitchen sink.

93

 "Hello?" He called. "Ashani? Are you there?"

His empty words reverberated against the chambers of my heart, echoed and vibrated into nothingness.

"No," I whispered. He had never loved me at all.

I turned the faucet on and walked away, thankful as I noticed the numbness tingling up from my toes.

What a week before Aunt V, indeed.

Nine

When I was getting ready to move in with my Aunt Virginia and Uncle Darrell, I realized I didn't know them very well at all. I had always liked them, however. They were a cute couple and I had always admired the way my aunt carried herself. There was something a bit regal about her. Nevertheless, we hadn't had any in depth conversations or spent any one on one time together. We had seen each other at birthdays, Thanksgiving and Christmas, sure. But that doesn't really make for getting to know someone.

I did know enough about her to know that she was my favorite aunt, however. She was funny, sure of herself, smart, and alluring in a way that made you curious about where she had gotten that blouse or that necklace. When you asked, she always had some delightfully exotic answer, like in the Galapagos or on the cruise to Alaska. She talked about life and travel like they were delicious and the passion was infectious. It seemed she walked around with her heart wide open, constantly receiving and giving. I remember once when Akin and I were very young I overheard her in tears telling my uncle Darrell about what a hard time Akin was having adjusting to his new medication and that she was worried about me. I decided then that I liked her very much.

My mother and I arrived at my aunt's house the next evening. I had brought a suitcase full of clothes, toiletries, and a few decorations in tow.

Eric's bed now had a rather lovely purple comforter with

matching throw pillows on it and a big potted plant on the bed side table. I thought it was the prettiest room I had ever seen. It seemed like my room now.

"Well, why don't you get unpacked?" my mother suggested. She seemed sadder than usual which meant her voice had to strain harder to get that cheery sound out of it she fought so hard to maintain.

I only did it because of that tired look in her eye. I would much rather do something like that in private and I was annoyed that now I had to pull out my underwear and bras in front of everyone, everyone being my aunt, and my mother. I may or may not be a touch on the dramatic side.

I tried to shield the suitcase with my body as I opened it and immediately stuffed the undies down to the bottom.

I put up the few picture frames I had brought with me on Eric's desk. Akin and I as babies in a park. My dad and I at the neighborhood 4th of July block party five years ago.

"You didn't bring any pictures of me," my mom pretended to pout.

I fumbled to find the right words. "Well, I can see you any time I want."

She seemed satisfied enough with that.

Aunt V smiled softly and showed me where she had cleared out space for me to hang my clothes.

Missy and Ginger, the dogs, were wandering around the house, but only Missy was truly interested in what all the commotion was about. Ginger was a beautiful golden retriever, who although not the sharpest tool in the shed, was a sweet old girl. Missy, on the other hand, was the smart as a whip little mutt who could herd a bunch of sheep, defend you to the death and read your mind.

I began hanging up my jeans and mostly purple tops when Missy appeared on my left. She was looking up at me with a tennis ball in her mouth. I smiled down at her. Sweet girl, I said in my head. I went back to my suitcase to get my sneakers out and place them on the floor of the closet. Missy stayed where she was and watched me make a few rounds from suitcase to closet when she decided she would also like to contribute. She took a few steps into the closet and gingerly placed her ball next to my neat row of shoes. I'm not sure if she meant much by it or if she thought we were playing a game and I was trying to teach her something, but it brought tears to my eyes. I felt welcomed and at home for the first time.

Ten

Therapy didn't start until the day after next, so when I woke up sometime around mid-afternoon the next day, my Uncle Darrell was already gone to work and it was just me and Aunt V.

I found her in the kitchen reading a book about soul types.

"So," she smiled, dainty turquoise earrings dancing near her shoulders. "Are you hungry?"

"Yes," I smiled too. "Very."

"Well, let's get out of here," she announced.

We sat at a Mexican food restaurant and talked for hours. I felt safe with her.

We ended up driving a good portion of the Pacific Coast Highway, well passed my usual Zuma and Malibu haunts. I relished the view and smell of the salty air. It was November so the breeze was chilly, but southern California has a way of letting any rain-free day be a perfect beach day in some way or another. We donned our coats and called some beautiful slip of beach all ours for the day. Missy bounded around along the shoreline and we walked and talked until the orange and pinks of the sunset inspired our quiet.

It was the first bit of peace I had had for as long as I could remember. I fell asleep in the car on the ride home.

I woke up the next day, anxious about therapy. The experience with Dr. Bastard had left a bad taste in my mouth. To say the least. Yet, I was hopeful and Aunt V was with me; I knew she wouldn't let anything bad happen to me.

The Rape Treatment Center of Santa Monica was on Santa Monica Boulevard, across the street from the flashy Mercedes Benz dealership and if you stood in the middle of the street you could see the Pacific.

Primo property, I thought to myself as Aunt V and I got out of the car. It was early in the morning and the air was a bit foggy.

We got off the elevator and a secretary greeted us before we even made it to the desk.

"Hello," she seemed older than your average secretary. I noticed this as she compiled a clip board of forms for me to fill out. "Good morning, darlin'."

I looked down at all the questions and immediately felt overwhelmed.

"Do I have to do this now?"

"Here," Aunt V took the clipboard. "Let me see."

She put on her reading glasses and glanced over the forms, making check marks here and scribbles there. I felt so grateful.

"Shadé?"

I looked up to see a woman in her late 60s wearing a sharply tailored chartreuse suit with chunky, funky topaz jewelry on her neck and wrists. She seemed to be wearing a full tube's worth of mascara and her entire collection of cocktail rings on at least nine fingers. She looked a bit batty, but I couldn't stop myself from liking her right away.

She was a character. And I've always liked women who weren't afraid to be seen and heard amongst the sheep.

"Hi, I'm Christine," she smiled and extended her hand.

"Hi, Christine," I took her hand. "I'm Shadé."

We walked into her office which was really more like a living room.

It was spacious and well decorated with two big plush couches, tall plants and weird art all over the walls.

I liked it in there. I felt like no matter what I said Christine wouldn't judge me. She was a little weird too.

She smiled and let me take in the room and when I asked if I could sit my bony butt on her decorator pillow she said, "Honey, you can do whatever you wanna do."

I was sold.

"So why don't you tell me about yourself."

I thought for a second and then decided to simply babble, "I'm Shadé. I'm 16. I was in the 11th grade but not anymore. I loved Europe and I want to go back without that lame student group. I don't play sports anymore. I wish I had stuck with ballet. I was a beauty queen once. My dad is an escape artist and my mom is trying to pretend like he's coming back. My brother. I don't even know where to start with that. He's heaven and hell all at once. I feel tired. And angry. All the time. Sometimes I take it out on myself."

"What do you mean by that?"

I swallowed. What was the RTC's policy on self harm?

Was I gonna get locked up somewhere? I figured best to leave it out and not traumatize the next patients by having to be violently escorted off to some less delightfully decorated psych ward through the waiting room. Because I would so not go willingly.

"Well, I mean...I'm mean to myself. I scrub really hard in the shower and I say mean things to myself in the mirror sometimes."

"Like what?"

"Like that I'm ugly and stupid and no one's gonna love me."

"Do you cut yourself?"

"I used to."

So much for keeping that cat in the bag.

"Not anymore?" She scribbled fiercely, quickly in her notepad.

"No," I reported firmly, which was true.

She seemed to believe me and we moved on.

"Back to being mean to yourself, why do you think you do that?"

I was quiet for some time as I thought about it.

"Because I'm mad at myself." I finally decided was the best reason. "Because I didn't fight back."

"Well, that's not what I heard," Christine smiled and danced her eyes around the room like we were sitting in the bleachers of the Hart High vs Canyon High football game, gossiping about who got caught making out in their car in the parking lot by security. "I heard you fought like hell, kid."

"I did kick him," I said, smiling in spite of myself. "He pushed me into a closet; when he was on top of me, he lifted himself up to try and unbuckle his pants. So when he was, like, off me, I kicked him really hard. Right in between the legs. He fell on his head."

"Good for you!" she crowed and let out a big woop.

I laughed.

Within fifteen minutes, she had not only gotten me to tell the story of my assault, but had figured out a way to make me paint my role in that story as more than a survivor: I was a conqueror. I never knew I had kicked his ass, but it sure felt good to know it now. Christine beamed at me and I basked in knowing that someone was proud of me. I felt proud of me too actually. It's amazing what a little perspective can do for you.

"You protected yourself. You didn't let him win in that closet. So I'm sure as hell not gonna let you let him win now."

She was determined and full of feminist sisterly support for me.

"It's not really up to me. It's up to you. But if I have any say, we're not going down."

I felt like we were going to burn our bras in a trash can and hoist up our picket signs any second now. I was so energized. I was going to get my life back. The realization sparkled over me. I wasn't going to be a high school dropout or a cutter or a teen suicide statistic. I was going to be me again. Not the old me. And that was ok. A new me would be even better.

I went to see Christine three times a week, then two times a week, then once a week over the course of 9 months, intermixed with a psychiatrist who wasn't a douchebag and who also prescribed me Zoloft. It gave me back my appetite and took away what was left of my sex drive, which was pretty much a skipped heart beat during a Denzel Washington movie. No major sacrifice there.

I did EFT (Emotional Freedom Techniques) with my aunt and a specialist over the phone which literally stopped me from having those debilitating flashbacks on the spot. While doing a series of breathing exercise, I had to tap myself at specific points on my arms, face, and chest.

"Imagine his face," the specialist commanded. "Now tap your sternum until it feels right to stop."

Sounds totally bizarre, I know, but it was nothing short of a miracle. The technique is being used to treat PTSD nationwide now and is reporting unbelievable success in war veterans. I will always be an advocate for therapy, but I can't deny what EFT did for me.

I don't remember what exactly was said during each session or which session contained the quotables I cherish most. After probably hundreds of sessions, I won't kid myself to think I can date and time stamp any conversations other than the first one. However, I do remember that it was soon after our initial meeting that Christine diagnosed me with Post Traumatic Stress Disorder.

The nightmares, the jumpiness, the revulsion I felt at being touched, the bland, boring taste all food had taken on, the disinterest in school or any of my hobbies, the baggy clothes, the scorching steam and self-hatred-filled showers were all classic PTSD symptoms. She asked me a series of questions. I answered yes all across the board.

It felt strange at first. I have a psychological disorder. My brain didn't work the way normal people's brains did. When a healthy person sees a new bottle of lotion in their bathroom, they might wonder what it smells like or think nothing at all. When I saw a bottle of lotion during the year I kept quiet, I would become agitated and rush to put it in a cabinet or away somewhere I couldn't see it. I hated the thought of touching my own body, let alone rubbing in a moisturizing agent. I applied Calamine lotion with a cotton ball if my skin cracked in the winter. That was all a part of my PTSD. And everyone's PTSD is different because everyone's brain is different. Eventually, I welcomed the diagnosis; it was nice to know what was wrong with me.

So while living in a quieter, more supportive house definitely helped with all the hyper vigilant aspects of my PTSD, Christine and I still had to sort through why I chose this route to cope instead of another.

A lot of it had to do with learning about myself. How had my childhood informed my emotional processes? What parts of my past made the option of keeping quiet an obvious choice for me? It didn't take a genius to figure out that I had learned to bottle my hurt at a very early age in light of Akin's clearly more pressing health concerns. I was probably already naturally an introvert anyway, but then the parent who I was closest to evaporated into thin air and had unidentified women answering his cell phone.

Upon his leaving the financial state of the family dissolved to the point that both our homes would have to be sold, bankruptcy was inevitable and my family was crumbling under the pressure. I stopped eating and sleeping normally. I became obsessed with calorie counting because I wanted so desperately to feel in control of something. I signed up for as many extra curriculars and advanced classes as I could, but still couldn't get busy enough to stay out of that house for as long as I needed to, it seemed. I ran myself into the ground. And that was before I was assaulted.

It actually made some sense to me. I was starting to "get" me.

Somewhere around halfway through my sessions with Christine, she asked me if I was ready to file a police report.

I was unsure at first, but Christine said, "Any information you can give them, any tiny detail you can remember might help establish a pattern. And then another girl might have a real shot at bringing this bastard to justice. Because of what you tell them, it won't just be her word against his."

Sold.

I had seen enough Law & Order: SVU episodes to know that the defense attorneys made a habit of ripping apart the rape victim, bringing in dates she had had sex with "too soon," painting her as a confused, misguided, alcoholic whore to the jury. She always looks so bewildered and afraid, like it's happening all over again. I would screech out, "Objection! Objection!" from underneath my blankets on the couch in the den. But I truly wonder how those attorneys live with themselves. Any ammunition I could give that girl to defend herself against those soulless sharks, I would.

Eleven

My mom and Aunt V both came with me to my next session and the officer was there waiting when we all arrived at the RTC.

We didn't use Christine's room, which was a bit jarring to me at first. He and Christine were standing in front of a large meeting room with a long table and many chairs in it. It was a few doors before Christine's and I had never really given it a second glance before.

I sat down in a big swivel chair on wheels and he and Christine stood, leaning themselves against the meeting table.

This is fully weird, I remember thinking, as I spun myself around a few times.

"Shadé," Christine said sharply, as if to say "snap out of it."

I stopped spinning and introduced myself to the officer. A bit childlike of me I'll admit, but I was insanely nervous.

"This is Officer Givens," she began slowly. "He works with the Rape Treatment Center and is specially trained to take full and compassionate reports from our clients. Are you ready now?"

"Yes," I replied, sorry to have disappointed her.

"Hi, Shadé," Officer Givens said and smiled a bit. He was chubby and very pale and he didn't have his gun, which I decided was probably, totally against procedure and that he did it out of consideration for me. I was touched.

"So let's talk about the night of September 1st 2001."

"Let's," I said, calmly but meaningfully.

"You went to a birthday party."

"Yes."

"It was at a friend's house?"

"Well, sorta. It was Ryan and Robert's birthday. The whole class was invited. It was Ryan's parents' house. It's in Topanga Canyon and it's huge. My mom probably has the address."

"I have it here," he informed me. "Were people drinking at the party?"

"I didn't see anyone drinking or doing drugs. But I'm a dork. And you can pretty much assume that if a buncha rich kids are gathered together late at night, chaperoned or not, there's gonna be drugs and alcohol. I, however, did not partake in any such activities nor did I witness them. I had Sprite."

Christine smirked. The officer took notes.

"What events led up to the assault?"

"No events, really. It was like a blitz attack. Someone shoved me into a closet. I was trying to get my phone out to text my ride that I wanted to go home, actually. And then wham! Out of nowhere."

"Did you recognize this person?"

"No, I had never seen him before in my entire life and he does not go to either of my schools."

"How do you know that?"

"He's a recognizable person. He's tall. Very tall. And athletic. And blonde. He would be the hot guy. On some team. I would know who he was and probably loathe him if he went to either Hart or Chaminade."

"Can you describe him in any other ways? Eye color? Ethnicity?"

"He was Caucasian and I don't know what color his eyes were. Something way too light. Like icy blue or gray. He was wearing a hat that had some stupid brand name on it like Abercrombie and Fitch.

I paused for a moment, "Can you believe I was almost raped by a Republican?"

The officer fought a laugh, but I could tell I had won him over.

He cleared his throat, "Can you remember anything else about him? Did he say anything to you?"

"He didn't really say much of anything actually. He was sort of...out of it."

"Say more," he made a circular motion with his pen to indicate that I should elaborate.

"He was fumbly and he couldn't get his pants undone. He pushed on me to hold himself up a few times, like he thought I was the ground. He also did a lot of like weird grunting and moaning. Not the pleasure-related ones but just like he was having trouble moving around. He also drooled on me. A lot."
Givens scribbled ferociously.

"Great job, Shadé," the officer said while flipping the top of his note pad back over then he shook my hand.

"Thanks," I replied, dryly. Do I get a gold star? I thought. "Great job" is a strange thing to say to someone after they've reported a rape to you.

"You should try calling some of your old friends. Someone might have invited him as a tagalong guest or someone else may have seen him and had a problem with him. If those parents were doing a good job chaperoning, they probably at least heard a story about some weird drunk kid stumbling around in their halls."

"But he didn't smell like liquor," I stated. "That's what was so weird. I don't know what he was on."

"But I'll call around," I promised.

When the officer left the room, Christine pulled me close to her and gave me a big hug. When I let go, I could see she had tears in her eyes.

"I'm ok, Christine," I said and smiled at her.

"I know you are," she smiled back, holding me out with her elbows locked so she could survey me with pride.

I opened the door to see my mom and aunt holding magazines they obviously weren't reading and waiting anxiously in the lobby.

"How did it go, Noon?" my mom asked from across the lobby, her voice pitched at the end.

"I did good," I told them both. "Let's go have lunch now."

"To lunch it is," Aunt V said, letting out a sigh of relief so big you'd have thought she was holding her breath the whole time I was in there. Maybe she was.

And off we went.

We decided on a hidden, little restaurant in Malibu called Paradise Cove. The view of the Pacific was gorgeous and you could sit right on the shore in these big wooden chairs with your toes in the sand. We ate. We laughed. They were really beautiful. My mom and aunt. And I was grateful to both of them. To my aunt for being one of the purest forms of love I had ever known and to my mom for acknowledging that I was better off in Santa Monica with my aunt at that time. I think that's how she's always loved me: figuring out ways to provide me with the tools to have a truly incredible life, even if she couldn't give those tools to me herself.

Over the course of those months of therapy and a few joint sessions together, I had begun to see a different side of my mother. She wasn't a mean mom who yelled at me for being forgetful and said hurtful teasing things I didn't think were funny. She was a woman, alone. With one extremely disabled son and a suicidal daughter. My father abandoned us, drained all of the accounts, and lost everything that she had ever worked for. She had to strap us to her broken back and walk. She picked probably the worst husband, short of an incestuous pedophile and to top it all off, she could never exercise, walk for long periods of time, or lift anything heavier than five pounds again. Let alone do the job she so desperately loved. I saw her hurt and frustration at my father's refusal and possibly inability to help her do just about anything. And I started thinking, I probably would've been yelling at Daddy, too, if he was my husband.

Her anger wasn't even really about me. She wanted me to have and be the best. She wanted me to be responsible, trustworthy, and strong. She wanted to push me, insure that I had the tools to live a successful life and was humble enough to acquire the expertise of others. She wanted me to see the world even if it wasn't by her side and she wanted to make damn sure I didn't end up in a marriage like hers.

When I look back at my favorite memories in my teens, her smiling face is always there, in the audience or by my side, eyes glistening with tears, glowing with pride. She supported everything I ever wanted to do and invested her time and energy to make sure I could do my best. As I boarded the plane for a summer in Europe that she had planned and paid for, I realized she had maintained an energy and enthusiasm for weeks that would've made you think she was going too. She was so excited for me. For my life. I was starting to really appreciate her, see her for who she was and all that she had done behind the scenes in my life. To her, I attribute much of my success. I was beginning to understand the way that she had always loved me very much.

Twelve

I waited some time before fulfilling my promise to Officer Givens but I finally decided that one lazy summer afternoon was the right time and I called some of my old Chaminade classmates.

I called Lily first.

She was shocked. "What? I was practically with you that whole party!"

Ryan had no idea who that guy was.

"I'm so sorry, Shadé. Really. So sorry."

I must have called ten other kids and asked them about that guy. My mom called Ryan's parents and spoke to them. No one knew anything. No one remembered seeing a guy who looked like that. No one remembered anything.

And the next day in therapy, it hit me like a ton of bricks: "that guy" probably didn't remember me anymore than my classmates remembered him.

I was sitting in a rape treatment facility, taking a year out of my life, risking my college admissions chances, talking about what happened in a closet for ten minutes or one hour for all I knew and he probably didn't even REMEMBER ME.

Christine and I were nearing the end of our time together. We could both feel it. I was getting stronger every day. She took me by the shoulders in one of our last sessions and breathed fervently, "Don't you dare. Don't you dare let something that was ten minutes in his life be the rest of yours. You've got too much to give, Shadé."

I took a deep breath in and felt the weight of her words. I did have too much. Too much to waste. Too much to throw away. And much too much to sit idly by and let someone take from me.

My Rape Treatment Center "graduation" was coming up. It's a huge fundraiser brunch held in a very generous donor's gigantic estate in Beverly Hills. Speeches are made. Hors d'oeuvres are served. Diplomas are handed out to clients who don't desire an extreme level of privacy and all the funds raised go to keeping counseling services free at the RTC.

Christine extended an invitation to me and said, "You can invite yourself a table's worth of supporters. You're gonna need it since you'll be a keynote speaker."

I looked down at the invitation; it was lavender and blue with embossed print on it and a dark purple ribbon. It was beautiful. Finally the letters came into focus. "Co-hosted by Jennifer Aniston and David Schwimmer" I was 16 and "Friends" was still so awesome back then. I felt like my heart was going to beat right out of my chest.

"Thank you, Christine," I burst out. "Oh thank you, thank you, thank you. I'm beyond excited."

"Three to five minutes," she said, peeling my arms from around her neck. "Talk about before, during, and what you're looking forward to after the RTC."

"I choose five," I giggled. "Five minutes. I've got a lot to say."

114

I rehearsed and rewrote for weeks. Candy probably heard that speech a thousand times. And the day of the brunch finally came. Mom, Aunt V, Uncle Darrell, their son Eric, my friend Daniela and I all made it down to frankly the most gigantic piece of Los Angeles real estate I've ever seen. The home was really more like a museum and the event took place in a series of huge white wedding tents on the front lawn that was longer and wider than 3 by 5 football fields. Did I mention that it was on the Miracle Mile and overlooked the entire valley? I had never been to a Beverly Hills $1000 a plate fundraiser-brunch. Let alone spoken at one. Good thing I didn't know any of these details before hand or I might have had the sense to be nervous.

We took our seats and were served an incredible meal. Christine took to the podium about half way through and one speaker from the LAPD discussed the efforts they were making in sensitizing their officers to rape survivors' needs and why that reporting process is different than say, a robbery or a non-sexual assault. Next, Christine introduced a young man. I knew I was up after him. I had never met him before but I felt like I already knew him. I suppose we already had one thing in common.

He began his speech, "My first day at the Rape Treatment Center was like a big hug." I burst into a smile. He seemed so sweet, so innocent, even child-like. He was small-framed and his hand gestures were slightly effeminate. When he told the story of his mother's boyfriend's sexual abuse, my eyes filled with tears. Who could do such a thing to this gentle, kind boy? He said he wanted men to know that their masculinity and sexuality were not in question because they were assaulted. He wanted more to be done to encourage male victims of rape to come forward. I had never even thought about male rape. He obviously had a point.

I stood up and clapped for him as hard as I could. I had almost forgotten I was about to speak next.

"And now, I'd like to ask one of our clients, Shadé Ogunleye, to come forward and tell us her story," Christine announced. "Please welcome, Shadé."

I strode to the podium, feeling confident.

I pulled the microphone up to meet my six foot stature and looked out at the audience. My mom and Aunt V were glowing. Jennifer Aniston smiled at me and I beamed back.

I cleared my throat, "I didn't want to accept what had happened to me. I thought if I buried it down deep enough, I could make it go away. But I couldn't and I lost my sanity trying to dig that hole." I revealed that which I had been keeping a dark secret to a tent full of strangers and I had never felt more comfortable.

My speech was probably longer than five minutes after all was said and done, but I felt like it was perfect. I got a standing ovation and David Schwimmer started it. I floated down off the stage. I was so proud. I had come so far. It was one of the most beautiful and memorable days of my life.

Everyone was still standing as I made my way back to the table where my family was. People told me how moved they were, how brave I was. It was such an incredible feeling.

"You are so beautiful... just so, so beautiful," Jennifer Aniston gushed when she walked over to me. She was impossibly petite and yet exuded a warmth and ingenuous kindness that was easily twice her size. She held my gaze in a way that let me know she meant so much more than physically beautiful. She had tears in her eyes when she reached to give me a tight hug.

Behind Jennifer, there was a similarly small woman with wiry gray hair peeking through her wild dark brown curls. There were tear tracks streaked through her makeup and her voice shook when she began.

"Thank you. Thank you. You just changed my life. I have never told anyone I was raped. It was almost 30 years ago now and I realized when you were speaking that I have PTSD too. I didn't think it even mattered anymore, but it does. It so clearly, clearly does. For me, for my husband, for my children. I'm so grateful and I'm going to get help now."

It took every ounce of my will not to cry. She was probably my mother's age and had never told anyone what happened to her. She had lived half of her life with PTSD. I was silent for a year; the thought of thirty years alone with that pain was unfathomable to me.

I squeezed her hand and gave her a hug. "I'm so glad," I whispered to her.

I watched her walk away and felt unable to move. Then it dawned on me.

This. This moment. This was my destiny.

I felt connected to myself and my purpose in a way I never had before. I thought to myself, what if, because I was brave enough to tell my story, someone else decided to get help and changed their life?

The answer was obvious to me. Then my own life would have been worthwhile.

I felt engaged, excited, sure of myself, and I couldn't wait to start school again. I wanted to prove myself. To myself.

My mom, Daniela, and I had spent a portion of the summer gallivanting across the country looking at colleges. UC Berkeley, Stanford, Emory, University of Michigan, Harvard, Boston College, Columbia, and NYU. The second I walked on to Columbia's campus I knew I was home. I loved everything about it. The Core Curriculum. The buildings. The professors whose classes I sat in on were brilliant. The students I saw and spoke to seemed like me. It was love. It was New York City. I had never wanted anything so badly in my entire life.

I covered my room with posters of Columbia. I made a goal sheet on a giant poster board and put it on my closet so it would be the first thing I saw when I woke up in the morning. I typed up a report card and an SAT score card and I envisioned myself getting straight A's and 100 points higher than the minimum SAT score Columbia required. I meant business.

School started and I put my nose to the grindstone. I was in every Advanced Placement or honors class I could get my hands on and I never stopped studying. I got all A's that first semester. I was back.

When it came time to fill out my Columbia application, I began nearly three months in advance. I painstakingly considered every word. Wrote. Rewrote. Hounded my teachers and school counselors about my recommendation letters. As per her usual method of operation, my mother hired a Harvard educated former English teacher to help with my application essays. She was an incredibly brilliant woman who helped me polish those few paragraphs into things of beauty.

I applied early decision, meaning if I got in, I was committed to going. There was nowhere else I wanted to go. I applied halfheartedly to some University of California system schools. The essays I had written for Columbia would have to do. I refused to put any heart into any other applications. Why was I a good fit for UCLA? I wasn't. 250 words on what I could add to UC Berkeley's community. Uhhh. My non-profit organization experience? Great. 246 words to go. I had literally no desire to go anywhere else. My safety school would have to be my mother's couch if I didn't get in to Columbia.

I was a little obsessed, I know. I was more nervous for my interview with a Columbia alumnae than I was to read my diary to half the cast of *Friends* and a hundred Beverly Hills socialites.

118

Halloween passed. Still no word from Columbia. Thanksgiving. Still nothing. I checked my email, the mail box, the voicemail religiously. Multiple times a day. I'd call my Nana from school and ask her to check the mail for me. I probably drove her and my mother nuts.

Then somewhere around the beginning of December I got an email from Columbia with the subject line, "Admissions Decision." My heart was pounding out my chest. Oh God. I didn't get in, I thought. They would've written, Welcome to Columbia or something like that. I was crying before I could even get my sweaty hand to click on the email.

An AOL email protection message popped up.

"This email contains images that might be harmful to your computer. Are you sure you want to open this email?"

"Oh my God!" I screamed at the computer. "LET ME OPEN MY EMAIL!"

The dial-up signal jerkily reloaded the screen and the words, Columbia University in the City of New York, were elegantly surrounded by Old English crowns to pay homage to the former name King's College.

I scrolled down to see the word, "Congratulations!"

I don't think I read any further than that. I clamped my hand over my mouth and cried.

All my hard work. All the late nights. The reading glasses. The movie nights, football games and parties I skipped. The millions of flash cards and sores on my wrists from being perched on the keyboard. The embarrassment I felt coming back to school a year behind my peers. The hundreds of hours of therapy. It was all worth it. I was going to be a Columbia Lion and I was elated.
I practically knocked the chair over so I could get enough space

to spastically sing out to the empty house, "I did it! I did it! I got in!" I jumped up and down, laughing and wiping away tears of joy, for at least twenty minutes. I called my mom first and she immediately started to cry too, "Ohhh, Shadé," she sniffled. "I'm so happy for you!" I couldn't stop smiling. I called my aunt, my tutor, my sister. For at least a month, I could just think of that word, "Congratulations!" underneath the Columbia letterhead and a joy so strong would shake me from my inner core and come bubbling out in a Cheshire cat grin and then outright giggles of glee.

My mom was so proud of me and our relationship had taken a turn for the better. I had started being more honest with her about what I was feeling and she had begun expressing herself in a way that helped me understand her. I was proud of her too.

I wanted to go to Columbia right then and there. The thought of another semester at Hart High was way too much to ask in my opinion. I wore my Columbia gear to school with my head held high and won the speech competition to deliver the graduation address to the class of 2005.

With nearly 1,000 students in the class, the football stadium was packed with nearly six times that many people. My sisters were in the audience too.

I ended my five year long high school career with a Ralph Waldo Emerson quote my father had taught me when I was a little girl, "do not go where the path may lead, go instead where there is no path and leave a trail." I felt like my life was beginning, like I was being remade in that thunderous applause.

Thirteen

I moved into my dorm at Carman Hall the following September a changed girl. I was softer, calmer. I didn't have to fight every day. I wasn't constantly offended, oppressed, or ostracized. I could be myself and making friends was a lot easier than I thought.

I was a nineteen year old freshman when I took proud steps onto Columbia's campus for the second time. No one even asked or cared why I was a year older than most freshmen. There were fifteen year old Sri Lankan geniuses and twenty-one year old Spanish missionaries who had taken time off to spread the Gospel in South Africa.

I loved Columbia. It was the hardest thing I had ever done. I was pushed harder than I ever was in my life, and that first year saw many sleep deprived inspired tears, but I still wouldn't trade it for anything. I finished my freshman year a better writer, a better student, and I believed I could figure out almost anything. Just give me the work. Astrophysics, Shakespeare, Biochem, bring it on. I finished believing I had, if not the personal knowledge myself, the ability to tap into the appropriate resources to figure out the problem. It was an incredibly empowering feeling. I felt like I belonged and like I deserved to be there, amongst some of the most brilliant young minds in the world.

It was easy to focus on academics in the Ivy League, but as sophomore year got under way, I realized, I wanted to date.

I had tried to date after the assault in high school but I wasn't ready. I met someone after graduation and we tried to do long distance from New York to Los Angeles. It was hell from start to finish. There was always fighting, jealousy, possessiveness, the desire to control me. Looking back, I realized that my two boyfriends up until that time had some pretty frightening similarities. I hadn't made that connection yet so when I started dating again, I didn't think to address my Daddy abandonment complex before I texted back that guy I met at the deli on 114th.

Anyway, I was supposed to be fixed. I thought I was supposed to be normal now. The Rape Treatment Center had handed me that diploma and it meant that I was a well-adjusted member of society again.

Right?

So I thought. Or perhaps, so I desperately wanted to believe.

Christine and I had tackled a host of issues other than the actual assault. My brother, my mom, my tendency to bottle then explode rather than express myself when something I don't like is happening. We only briefly touched on what my father's abandonment of our family had done to my ability to trust men, or love myself in general, let alone view my self-worth within a relationship. It is a specific kind of self-worth, in my opinion. I felt like a million bucks in my 16th Century English Poetry class, but across the dinner table from a cute guy, I didn't have a gauge for myself.

Truth is, at twenty years old I didn't know who I was well enough to pick out a person that would be a good match for me. I just went out to dinner with whoever asked as long as I thought he was attractive. Dinner on Friday? Sure beats the hell out of the dining hall. So off I went all dolled up, date after date. Some lasted longer than others. Three dates. Six months. Two years. Inevitably I had to come to terms with the fact that I was dating the same person over and over again. If you teach people how to treat you, I was handing out the wrong lesson plan.

I was putting on this "I'm a baby" act and dating much older men. I demanded their constant help, reassurance, even discipline. "What should I do? What do you think? Is it ok if I...?" I needed ceaseless attention. I needed to know, without a shadow of a doubt, that I was their number one priority and that they would never leave me. I would act out and throw hours-long crying, pouting fits if I felt even the tiniest bit slighted. He needs to get off the phone because he's at work right now? Well then, I would beg him to leave the building and talk to me for just five more minutes.

I was always testing, pushing to see how far he would go for me, how much he loved me. A totally acceptable way for a toddler to behave towards her father as he drops her off at preschool for the first time when she wants to make a pit stop for an ice cream cone. A completely insane way for a young woman to relate to her partner, who eventually becomes confused when she simultaneously demands to be controlled and respected. I had no idea what a boyfriend was supposed to be or do. Weren't they just supposed to make everything better?

I had become addicted to being with someone. I wanted the comfort of a relationship. Sex was irrelevant to me. I just wanted someone there for me, to love me unconditionally. I hopped from boy to boy to boy, annoyed if they wanted me to sleep with them. Sometimes I'd take only a few days off in between two. After whatever obviously deranged healing process I deemed was over, I would essentially, call, "Next!"

I was so broken inside and I couldn't even see it. I figured it was all their fault. They just didn't love me like I needed to be loved. Either they didn't know how or they didn't want to. Whichever of the two was the crux of the problem was of no particular concern to me. Clearly, I wasn't doing anything wrong. So forget them. Oh, and....next!

I hadn't yet grown tired of the revolving door I was pushing through at turbo speed when a phone call from my friend Chloe stopped me dead in my tracks.

Fourteen

I wrote a poem the day after Chloe called to tell me she had been raped. A man rang the doorbell, appeared to be drunk or high, and asked for her mother. She wasn't home. He pushed his way into the house and pulled a knife on her. He held her down and forced her to have sex with him. He couldn't finish, became flustered and stumbled twice before he let himself out the front door.

Never to be seen again.

Chloe lay on the floor, unable to move until her mother came home from work to find her there. Frozen.

I wrote these words in agony over my powerlessness. Over the seemingly choking omnipresence of rape. Chloe was the fifth of my friends to make a weeping phone call to me that struggled to begin, "Day...something happened..." I kept my composure for Chloe when she called, gave her the tools that had saved me: phone numbers to the rape treatment center in Santa Monica, an EFT specialist to stave off the impending torture of Post Traumatic Stress Disorder, and a request that she take time off of school and get out of that house. She sounded hallow. We prayed together and I told her she would be ok. My voice didn't waver once. But when she hung up, I screamed as long as I could. Slumping into a heap on my dorm room floor, where I kicked, hit, and knocked over anything around me. Slamming my elbows, hands, toes. Feeling my bones against the wood of my desk and the plaster of the walls.

I ripped the posters off my wall and tore up any paperwork on my desk. I felt crazed, ravenous. I don't think I had ever allowed myself to process that emotion for my own rape. I was hurt, defeated, ashamed, depressed. But enraged? This was the first time. I had never been a physically aggressive person when I was angry, but I had bottled so much, for so long.

I imploded. Crying and screeching and ripping at anything that would tear in my claws. Exhausted, I sat down to make sense of my destruction. I didn't tell Chloe, but that was the first time I had prayed in years. It felt out of place in my life now. I wasn't really certain how to deal with the fact that I had just started automatically leading us in prayer in the middle of our conversation. Out of the corner of my eye I saw a piece of poetry I had attempted to shred from my Black Paris literature class. Edward Said. It began, pregnant with the pain of the psychological ramifications of slavery, "But I am the suffering."

And so did I.

But I am the suffering.
After trying to wedge your penis out of the valve of my aorta,
I come to terms;
You have fucked me.
But I am the failure.
For it was my duty
To save, to protect, to hold.
I wanted so desperately
To carry this burden myself.
To be the only one.
All the while knowing
this vain hero's cape would make a mockery of me.
To sacrifice would have been my glory.
Had I been there, I would have fought.
Had I been there, I would have bled.
I would have sobbed--empty, bottomless, birth-giving sobs.
I would have died for my daughter.
For her.
For you.
But I am the shattering.
Remnants of WHO I wanted to be in the face of my opponent.
Undefeatable. Inevitable. Bastardizing abomination in the face of
God.
Do you know what you took from me?
What you take from me.
How dare you? You coward!
Show your face!
Show me your face!
Show me how you slithered out the door homogenizing into our
indecent world,
But I am the suffering.

127

Finally, I began to process why I was so angry.

They were all free.

My rapist had never been brought to justice. I couldn't identify him if he was sitting next to me on the plane as I type this very sentence. Even if the trial had gone horribly wrong, even if the defense attorney had found some implied nudes of me online and the uptight jury had turned on me, at least I would have put my hand on the Bible and told the world what he was. But I had never gotten that chance. Instead I had been left in a prison of my own madness. Serving time in my mind.

And it wasn't fair. It was injustice in its cruelest form.

They were never brought to their knees to wretch on the floor and cry out to God, "Mercy, mercy, mercy please, Father. I'm begging you to take this from me." They had never questioned their sanity. With the luxury of freedom, they were untouched.

Melissa's was the first to escape.

Her rapist attacked her in a parking lot. Not enough physical evidence.

Tai's step father's statute of limitations had run out. He had stopped raping her when she hit puberty. Tai had gained the courage to tell someone at 17.

Michelle's ex-boyfriend was a married and decorated officer in the Marines. With a child. Plus it would be my word against his, she had sighed.

Alyssa was pulled into a van, blindfolded, beaten, and penetrated with foreign objects after she decided to end her none-too-romantic adventure with a bad-boy, gang affiliated boyfriend. She couldn't voice-identify anyone.

Then Chloe called and I broke.

I realized as a society how we are approaching rape is not working. We seem to be sarcastically saying, "What is rape, anyway?"

Why do we tell young women, "Don't get raped"? Why don't we tell young men, "Don't rape!"? If one in six women in the United States reports being raped, how many more are keeping quiet? How many more are too afraid? Too close, perhaps even too in love with their rapists to speak up? And more importantly it would seem how many men are rapists? Why aren't those statistics making headline news? How many men don't know what the actual definition of consent is? And furthermore, why are they angry enough to commit such a heinous act in the first place? To hold someone down while they sob and scream for their life is a far greater crime in my mind than even armed robbery. How do they stay aroused and why?

Why don't we preach that a woman has the right to drink as much as she'd like, wear whatever she wants, do any dance move that suits her fancy; and as a matter of fact, she can do gymnastic tricks on a pool table and belt out, "I'm a whore!" with the help of backup dancers in cone-bras, but YOU don't have the right to touch her.

For some reason, we tell women to be hyper vigilant, guard their drinks with their lives, bring a flashlight or weapon that can fit into a fashionable clutch with an easy-to-open snap, and to use the buddy system on a girls' night out. Pardon me, but does that safety spiel remind anyone else of when the counselors gave instructions to go to the bathroom at sleep away camp in the woods? Since when are men the mental and physical equivalent of WILD BEARS? Our best bet is to flash a light in their eyes, run away in a zigzag and scream for our buddy to go get help?

We're not dealing with other rational beings apparently. A police officer in Canada was quoted saying, "Women should avoid dressing like sluts" in order to avoid being raped. http://www.bbc.co.uk /news/world-us-canada-13320785

Two NYPD officers were acquitted of rape after confessing to either witnessing or actually "cuddling" nearly naked with a woman in her bed after walking her home. She was visibly intoxicated, which to my mind, means she was unable to consent to anything, let alone "cuddling" with a stranger while someone else watched it happen. They were on duty. To serve and protect indeed.

Common sense and safety aside, why shouldn't I be able to do whatever I damn well please? I was coming to terms with the plain and simple fact: I don't feel as free as a man does and my culture is informing that feeling.

If any man reads this I humbly ask you to consider that you most likely have absolutely no idea what it's like to walk through this life as a woman, to simply walk down the street, to move to a new neighborhood, to have a drink at a bar with a few friends, to travel to other countries, to have sex. It's different for us. We consider things perhaps you don't. For example, am I safe here? Not should I move my wallet to my front pocket or maybe I'll drag the big screen in when less people are watching. Am I SAFE? We think it; we feel it; it radiates over our entire beings when you walk behind us in a parking lot, tell an off-color joke, or offer us a drink we didn't see the bartender make.

At any given moment, we might be questioning our safety. You don't have to understand it. But if you could respect it that might help us to stop feeling like we're in a pitifully outmatched, yet somehow annoyingly constant fight: Girls Scouts versus roaring, Jeep top-tearing, ice cooler-smashing, literally foaming at the mouth savage brutes. So when we do decide to take off our badge-filled sash and skirt for you, feel free to celebrate knowing that we don't see you as one of the beasts. Further, feel free to keep proving to us that whatever taming process you went through is still working.

I called Psychological Services on campus the very next day and booked an emergency appointment. I started peeling back the layers of the damage my father's absence had done. There was so much more than I had ever anticipated.

I hadn't recovered from that day I had watched him board the plane to Abuja, Nigeria at LAX when I was 13 years old.

I had moved on in so many other aspects of my life, but emotionally, I was frozen right there at the point of trauma. I started going to therapy regularly over the course of the next two years in hopes of getting to the bottom of my "Daddy issues." I wanted so desperately to be in love, to have a healthy relationship. It didn't even occur to me that I needed to have a healthy relationship with myself first.

I thought Prince Charming would show up one day while I was gardening and singing beautifully to small woodland creatures. From there, we would ride off into the sunset together. Nobody ever told me that "happily ever after" took work. I could recall no scenes where Cinderella had to postpone the wedding so she could get her head straight in therapy about her father's sudden death and step mother's abuse.

I was at a total loss. What was love, if not a knight in shining armor to rescue you from your current miserable life?

I had no idea I was supposed to rescue myself. I spent two years learning how to take care of me, what tools to use if I felt myself getting depressed, how to eat healthy, how to manage my anger, and how to express myself to others. I had no idea how to do any of those things. While I eventually came to enjoy time spent alone cultivating my hobbies, I remember feeling annoyed by how much work I had to do before I could date again. Sad and funny, but true.

My therapist and I did a few joint long distance phone sessions with my father on three-way and immediately, the main issue was disturbingly clear. When my father didn't pick up our first few attempts at a call or missed a session all together, I would become absolutely irate.

"Why are you upset, Shadé?" my therapist would try gently.

"Why do you think I'm upset?" I snapped. "My dad has known about this appointment for two weeks. I've reminded him more than once. And now, here it is. Here's the time. And he says it's so important to him. He wouldn't miss it for the world. Yeah? Well, he also said 'wild horses' couldn't keep him from my high school graduation and my move-in day here at Columbia. Ready for the big shocker? He missed both. He's so full of shit. Empty promises and fancy words to cover up the fact that the only person he really cares about is himself. He always protects and takes care of himself. He never prioritizes my needs. Ever. How am I supposed to feel about that? If this was a three-way phone call with the President of Nigeria and his secretary, he would've picked up the damn phone. Why am I not as important? Why doesn't he care?"

"In any abusive relationship there is always..."

"Wait," I cut her off to correct her. "My father never abused me. I was spanked a few times but it was never unjust and I wasn't afraid of my dad."

"Inconsistency is the most sincere form of abuse," my therapist replied quickly. "Don't underestimate it."

I took in her words and felt the weight of them. It was true. Had my father run off to Nigeria when I was thirteen and never once called or looked back I think I would've been better off. The true damage was done by the sporadic phone calls, the missed birthdays with broken promises of a surprise visit, or an email reminding me to look out for a package that never came.

His greatest crimes, to my mind, were the lies and how hard he worked to preserve himself by keeping my sisters and my mother and I apart. I'm not sure how he's supposed to answer for that and I still struggle with understanding why he did it.

I spent so much time on that couch, untangling the web of lies my father crafted to throw on to our family before he left for Nigeria. Trying to figure out what exactly the hell just happened could describe many a phone call between my sisters and I over the years. Despite being kept apart and told false stories, we still managed to love each other fiercely. I suppose if he had brought us all together in peace, he would have had to do right by my sister's mothers. Nevertheless, we fought for each other.

I remember the day it dawned on me that my sisters had been taken from me. I was probably around ten years old when I found a shoebox under my father's bed of newspaper clippings, highlighting Bunmi's track and field success, pictures of Kunmi on pointe in her tutu and tights, and letters I had written to my sisters. I didn't know their addresses and I had asked him to mail them for me. To this day, I don't understand why he would do that to me, to us, and our sisterhood. Why wouldn't he let me celebrate my sisters, their personalities, and talents?

I remember being confused, looking at the contents of that box. Who were these girls? Why didn't I know Kunmi was a dancer? Why hadn't anyone told me that she had dedicated her life to this art? I surveyed the series of pictures in awe. She exuded effortless grace. Her feet arched perfectly, her hands perched delicately above her head, her face angelic. I was stunned. All my father had ever told me about her was what a trouble maker she was, but here was this beautiful girl and I knew looking at her there, that he was lying.

Couldn't he see? All she wanted was peace, her family in the audience, and enough space to dance. Her eyes held the same pain that mine would, the same neglect and abandonment that made her graceful, gazelle-like demeanor a target. She was prey out there amongst predators and I would soon know exactly how she felt. Why wouldn't Daddy help her? She needed him. She needed her family. It was written all over her face; it was my face. Ten years later. I tucked one of the pictures into my pocket and prayed Daddy wouldn't notice.

I continued rummaging through the box and I picked up one of the many articles Daddy had clipped out. I was drawn to this one in particular because it included a relatively large picture; Bunmi was flying through the air, leg muscles contracted and glistening against the camera's flash, face intent, braids floating behind her. She was so beautiful, frozen in time like that. Seconds later, she would land in a sand pit and set the record for her high school. I felt a pang in my chest. I should have been there. I didn't even know this side of her.

When she came over during those years, there was so much tension raging through the house, neither of us could relax enough to be ourselves. Looking at her cheekbones and the way she held her face in that awkward teenage smile, I saw my face. She was my sister; I held the article gingerly and made sure none of my tears fell on the page. She was my sister and I didn't even know her. I wonder if my father knew how my sisters and I suffered without each other, the gravity of what he did to us and took from us.

While in college I realized how much we had lost, more than ever, because once I left that house we could call and see each other freely. They visited me. I visited them. It was as it always should have been. Their voices, their support, their love, simply, their presence in my life—undamaged by anyone's meddling— became my very life-force. The time before them seemed... incomplete.

And there it was, that word incomplete made too much sense. I thought my father had loved me more than anything in the world. But he hurt me, took from me, and made me feel incomplete when he left. I was using the way he treated me as the threshold, the definition of love, as well as the parameter by

135

which to measure the way others loved me. His abusive "love" had made me not only blind to know when others were abusing me, but I thought abuse was love.

"You're right," I whispered.

"My father has abused everyone I love," I stated flatly.

"What I would like for you to identify is a particular moment in your history with your father. There was an exact moment when you knew him to be who he is, when you knew your relationship with him could not evolve passed that point. But you violated the validity of that knowledge."

"I know exactly what moment that was for me," I didn't skip a beat.

"I was dying. I was six feet tall and 120 pounds. I couldn't eat. My hair was falling out and I couldn't grow my nails. Everything hurt. My bones hurt. I wasn't sleeping for days at a time. I was reliving the rape in my mind, multiple times a day, every day. I was cutting my arms, thighs, and wrists with a Swiss Army knife. And I begged him to come home. I mean, truly, I begged him to save my life. And he wouldn't. I don't think I've ever forgiven him for that."

"Ultimately, Shadé," she said meaningfully. "That's your decision to make. Forgiveness is a big word and it has many different definitions. You can forgive someone and let them go. You can forgive someone and speak to them once a year. But you have to set parameters and boundaries. You have to know what you want and what you deserve so that you know when you're being violated."

"Today was a violation," I retorted. "I would never do that. I would never tell my daughter I was going to be at a therapy session so we could heal our relationship and not have the common decency to show up or call or send a freaking pigeon.

Who does that?"

"So one of the things you value is that someone keeps their word to you," she wrote it down as she said it. "What else? Keep going."

"I want to feel like a priority to someone who loves me," I continued. "Because they are a priority to me."

"I want to know that I'm not alone," my voice shook. "I could never, ever hear the voice of someone I love breaking and say 'I can't.'"

"You didn't," she assured me. "You're here because you talked your friend Chloe through a sexual assault and gave her resources that are probably saving her life as we speak."

I reached for a tissue, "But I wanted to do so much more. I just wish I could do it for her. She's just a baby."

"She's five years older than you were when you were raped."

"That's true," I said slowly.

"And if she had the presence of mind to call you," she smiled. "She's probably a lot smarter and stronger than you're giving her credit for."

I smiled back, "Fair enough."

"I think that'll do it for today," she said. We still had a few minutes left in the session, but it had been a full enough 45 minutes on the couch for me as well.

"But I have an assignment for you," she stopped me as I made my way towards the door.

"Assignment?" I cringed. I had enough homework and reading to do tonight on top of the decompressing and extreme

137

caffeinating I would have to do to shake off this emotional exhaustion well enough to study for my Post-1940s American Fiction midterm.

"I want you to write a letter to your father," she said firmly. "What did you need from a father? Generic, broad, open statements. Then narrow it down. What did you need from him? Get specific to your shared experiences. What do you want from him now? What are the boundaries if you want him to be a part of your life? How has he hurt you and in what ways? Say it all. Get it all out. Curse. Tell your secrets. Tell his. Leave it all on the field. When you're done, you can decide if you'd like to send it, but write it like you won't."

The task sounded daunting at first, but I later understood as I shook out a hand cramp and flipped my journal to page six of my letter that I was finding the process cleansing and healing.

It wasn't my original intention, but the letter ended in a goodbye. I had nothing more to say to him. I was forming friendships I cherished deeply; my sisters and I were closer than ever and I had begun forming a healthy relationship with my mother.

My friend Shannon later pointed out that one of the principles of operant conditioning holds some relevant truths about learned behavior in abusive relationships, especially in the seemingly inexplicable and vicious cycle of domestic violence. It begins simply enough; a mouse learns that he receives a pellet if he pushes down on a lever inside his cage. He has been conditioned to push the lever in order to receive a treat. If the experimenter wants him to stop pushing the lever, he should permanently disengage the food pellet dispenser. The mouse will then stop pushing the lever in a relatively short amount of time. However, if the mouse pushes the lever and he has no way of determining whether or not he will receive a food pellet, he will push that lever for an extraordinarily longer amount of time than the mouse whose dispenser was permanently disengaged. The hope, the possibility of a pellet is at least worth a try every time.

I saw myself immediately as that little mouse. There I was, pushing that lever, over and over again. In hopes that maybe this time, my dad would come through for me. Last week, he called me right at 3pm on Wednesday and Sunday like we had agreed. This week, he missed both days all together. That inconsistency drove me insane. Maybe this time he would come to Christmas, to my graduation. Maybe this time he would remember my birthday. Maybe this time he would pick up the phone and go back to being my Daddy again. That hope, that slight chance kept me sick for almost ten years.

There was no way I would accept the way he was treating me from anyone else in my life. If he couldn't value me enough to pick up the phone once a week, I couldn't value him and respect myself at the same time. I deserved better than that. I deserved so much more.

Fifteen

The letter I wrote to him was deeply personal and not to mention terribly long; as such, I'm choosing not to share it in its entirety here.

I realized that the primary emotion I felt was disappointment. He had let me down. He demanded such an extreme level of intimacy in our every interaction. I had to be 100% present. Then without warning he would want nothing from me. Then everything again. And it dawned on me. I didn't have to be on this sick rollercoaster. It wasn't easy to say goodbye, by any means, and only my sisters truly supported my decision. People called me cruel for not picking up my father's calls.

"But he's your DAAAAD," they bleated at me.

"So?" I replied. "I should accept his abuse because what? Fathers and daughters go together? No matter what? I just learned this and maybe you need to hear it too. Romantic, familial, friendship, even umbilical cord bonds are worthless in the face of abuse. They mean nothing. I was lent to him by the universe and he had a duty to protect me. I don't owe him anything and I don't have to stay anywhere with anyone who repeatedly hurts me. I don't care who they are."

And so my letter was inspired.

Dear Daddy,

I never wanted it to be this way, but you've left me with no choice. You have forced me to choose between my self respect and my relationship with you. I've come too far to ever elect anyone or anything before my ability to look myself in the eye again. In some ways, I think you'd be proud of me for saying goodbye. The Daddy I remember would have said, "A man without his word is a man without honor" if I shared the promises you broke to me as if they were someone else's empty words."

It was on that very principle of a proverb he had taught me himself that I cut him out of my life. He called occasionally and left strange voicemails, begging me to forgive him, yelling at me to pick up next time he called, blabbering on about money that some project would soon yield, crying about the pain I was causing him. After a while, I stopped listening to the voicemails. They were always about him anyway. He never once said, "How are your classes? How are your friends? I miss you." When I wrote down that I had needed support from him, I realized he hadn't done that for me in a very long time. Just been there for me. Heard me out. Instead, he talked about himself, his hurt, his projects.

The lies he told and the deliberate way he demonized my mother to me in my childhood were directly responsible for the alienation I felt in our home when he left. And ultimately, was one of the primary reasons I didn't come forward when I was assaulted until I literally broke under the weight of PTSD. He took my mother from me. He gave me so much, but he viciously snatched it all back, piece by piece, and silently stole so much more in ways I was blind to for most of my life.

"...I don't want you to think I hate you. I don't. I love you very much. Some of my favorite memories are with you. How we used to laugh. And how much you taught me. I'm grateful. What I need you to understand is that each time you didn't show up, all the times you didn't call, each time you broke my heart, denied me, and hurt my siblings, I lost respect for you. Our relationship was based entirely on respect and trust. We have not one shred of either of those vital pillars upon which to rebuild a relationship left. There is nowhere to go from here..."

"I figure I should catch you up on my life since you never ask. I'm doing well in school. I love being an English major now. I dropped the idea of med school and I'm going to graduate school for public health next year. I think it'll be a much better fit for me. As for my love life, pretty non-existent since that horrible breakup a few years ago. It seems I haven't had my heart broken in a very long time actually. I've been thinking about heartbreak these days because a dear friend of mine is deep in the throes of it. You know the kind that literally tosses your whole world upside down? When you can barely make it to the bathroom for the crying, to open the fridge to think how much you want to throw up in the produce drawer and close it but you haven't eaten in days? Ahh yes...THAT kind. Eons ago or yesterday it seems, when you were in love, you would've killed for her, died for her, booked a next day one way ticket from LA to Tokyo with your last 3,000 dollars because you have to be young and broke to be in this kind of love. There is only you and her. Your heart's in a blender with the power switch on and she can press 'puree' with a word. It's the definition of vulnerability. It's beautiful; it's terrifying; it's everything you've ever wanted because all at once you're lost and at home, and understood and alive and so alone and certain you could die happy in her arms. Yeah, poor kid's got all the symptoms, and she says this was her second major heartbreak. I've had one. And I've been wondering if your heart ever breaks like it does the first time. I'm starting to realize that after the first one, I hardened in a way that didn't really let the others shatter me, smash me quite as exquisitely and totally as that first one did. It's all pretty blurry. That shattering.

The days run together, gray, indiscernible from each other in my frayed clippings of post-him. He consumed me. I couldn't believe how far in I had let our love. There was no piece of me, no dream, no cell I could find that didn't have him in it. Somehow, stealthy like he is, he had superimposed himself into my code. In losing him, I lost me too. I remember not getting dressed for days, having to take showers sitting on the floor, sobbing, not caring that the girl in the shower stall next to me could see my ass. And being the only halfie girl on the 5th floor of my dorm, it wouldn't have been a difficult ass to identify. I scared the hell out of my roommate. She grew weary of my psychosis, dirty oatmeal dishes, and creepy collages. I went to her wedding and I smiled for her but we don't speak. (I'm sorry, Steph. Our friendship was just another casualty of my crazy.)

I started piecing myself back together over the holidays. Nothing like a new year to get you all half-drunk sentimental about new beginnings. It was like...teaching myself how to function again. First I had to put my life back together in my head. I took Akin with me to Rite-Aid so I could buy some poster boards. You taught me that, Daddy. To put it all on paper and make a path for myself. It was easier in the 4th grade though.

One thing I love about my brother is how he knows me. You never got to know him very well. He was only 9 when you left. You missed out on how emotionally intelligent he became, the depth of his genius. I think he spoke to me twice in the month that I was home. Once was to say Merry Christmas and the other was to tell me as I sat there writing down my new dreams and goals, "You're gonna find your way out, big sis, ok?" I stared at him for a second and thought, "Thanks." Akin can always tap into my metaphor.

In finding my way out, I realized I made my love out to be something he wasn't in the beginning. He wasn't my saving grace. I had to be... with my scissors and glue stick and little brother by my side. I wanted him to make your wrongs right. I wanted him to heal me and create this perfect life together as an act of vengeance. I wanted "us" to be a "f*ck you" to you for turning my childhood into a cemetery of memories I wish I could keep buried. I wanted him to fill up my heart with new swells and waves that made me feel...like the most beautiful girl in the world. To him. That's how you used to make me feel. Like I was everything. But he was never capable of loving me like that. It wasn't his job or fault. It was yours.

You have failed me.

He was broken too and I couldn't fix him, no matter how much I wanted to. I wanted us to save each other as some grand testament to the awesome healing power of true love. But I had to learn how to save myself and be by myself before I could be with anyone. I chose broken people to love and accepted their abuse because you had taught me not only to believe I deserved that, but to believe that to be abused was to be loved.

As I put those pieces together, Akin sat next to me. Quiet, looking up at the stars, probably a little afraid as I fell apart next to him, but he sat there. A constant in the middle of my mayhem, to let me know I wasn't alone. Every day for a month.

I think I've always been looking, searching for love in a purer form than it's ever been shown to me by a man. But I already had it. All along. Your beautiful son was there to call "just to say I love you no matter what," to say, "you're the best and I know you can do it," to annoy me, to get me, to drive me nuts, to say nothing at all but just be with me.

After you left, Akin and I would sit on the swings in the back yard talking about where we would go if we could teleport.

"I vote for Paris," I'd begin.

"Where's that?"

"In France."

"Let's go to Africa instead."

"Where in Africa? It's not one place you know."

"Fine, smart-face. Nigeria."

"That's the only place you've already been. Let's go to Morocco."

"First Morocco, then Africa, then back home."

"But... oh, forget it. Where's home? Here?"

He shrugged and kicked sand on my shoes. "Duh. Wherever you and I want."

There is something so pure about your son. Even in the darkest moments, he is...all emotion. He is all heart, all love. He is so black and white, so literal, and serves as a constant to me, a reminder that there is goodness, there is truth, there is God, there is love. When he pissed me off when we were kids, Mom used to try to illicit my sympathy and say he would have a simple life. Just have his little job, his little family, his little house. That would be it. And I remember thinking how beautiful.

And I get to be a part of it. I can't believe I was chosen to be his sister. I'm not sure who I'd be without Akin, but I know I am a kinder, more compassionate, and more accepting version of myself because of him. He is and has always been the personification of the incredible name you gave to him: a warrior has returned. I had built up all these barriers against love as a kid to protect myself. But Akin fearlessly, lovingly has always broken through them, even when they were bigger than he was. And in showing me where they are he has offered me the most beautiful gift: the opportunity to love as he does. He showed me God's heart for me. He was a child blindly reaching into inconceivable darkness to pull me out. Akin is the reason I believe in God.

You know that saying, "Never forget that when life brings you to your knees, you're in the perfect position to pray." You sound so

146

sad in some of the messages you've left me. I'm sorry for the pain you're feeling. Sometimes you ask for my forgiveness and I want you to know that you already have it. I forgive you. But you might want to take up that guilt you're feeling with Him.

You're not alone without me. You don't ever have to feel alone. If you're half as brave as Akin, you'll be alright. Sometimes when I feel lonely, I read Psalm 27. My friend Karen gave me that Psalm and it has been a true gift to me. My favorite line is 27:10, "When your mother and father forsake you, I will take care of you." It's not "if" your mother and father forsake you," they will inevitably let you down. Even the people who are supposed to love you the most, will forsake you. If you feel like I'm forsaking you now like you did to me then, maybe you'll feel comforted to know that when you missed the flute recital where I led my section to regional honors, He was the first to stand up and give me a standing ovation for my solo. When mom and I went to the track and field Nationals where I qualified for the Junior Olympics, He held my hand before that last jump. When I was sitting in the bathtub, sawing away at my forearm with a razor, He sent Akin to bang down the door, jump in the tub with me, clamp his bare hand over my cuts and whisper, "Please don't hurt my arm anymore." When I was being raped in a closet, He was there too.

I know it's hard to understand. It was hard for me too. Believe me. I had a serious bone to pick with God about that one. But God chooses some of us to be refined by sorrow. Hallowed out, stripped of everything, sobbing on the bathroom floor, you just might find yourself purified, crying out to be made new, to be filled up by Him. To get closer to Him. To understand Him and what He wants for you. Not from you. For you.

I have a message, a purpose, a testimony, a wish for healing for this nation and our world. It's such a beautiful, invigorating, exciting feeling; it's hope. If I can go from a suicidal atheist to a believer with a cause in the space of a year, then anything's possible.

I pray for you, for your soul, for the darkness I know that tortures you. But it isn't my duty to ensure your soul's salvation and I don't have the power to help you forgive yourself. That's up to you."

I read that letter to my father when he invited himself to my college graduation. I saw my father for who he was. Took the rose colored glasses off and did a bird's eye view on his life with the facts I knew to be true. And I was horrified.

He had abandoned women and children for all of his adult life. The mothers of his children. His own, innocent flesh and blood. We were all cast aside. A parasite, who jumped from host to host, he never worked for very long and jumped ship whenever his gig was up. He was emotionally, financially, mentally, physically abusive and might have been a sociopath. But, he was my father, he was human and I had loved him.

So I decided to let him go.

I made some other decisions that day too. I decided I wasn't going to become what I had endured. My home would be nothing like the one I was raised in and my marriage would be nothing like my parents'. I wanted to be something other than what I had seen and to be someone other than who I had been programmed to be. I wanted to be gentle, loving, kind, patient, unselfish, giving. I wanted to be beautiful.

I wrote down the things my father had given me, the things I wanted to remember. My Nigerian culture, the few words in Yoruba I could recall, the century old proverbs, the folklore, and the silly memories. I let the rest of it go. I had to. If I didn't, I ran the risk of punishing my future partner for my father's mistakes, asking him to fill his shoes in some inappropriate way or shutting him out for fear of being perceived as too weak otherwise. I wanted a happier life than that.

148

Now, I was ready to explore the passions I had begun to cultivate, free from this sickness.

So I took some time for myself that summer after my junior year. My self-prescribed mission was to learn about myself. To learn what I liked, what I wanted to do, who I wanted to be, what brought me joy. And it didn't take me long to realize that I didn't lose those parts of myself to PTSD. My dad didn't pack them in his suitcase and cart them off to Nigeria either. I buried them, afraid to let my dreams come to light because they might outshine the comfort of the pain.

I hadn't had the mental space to refine my goals so I had pressed on through three years of college and the pre-med curriculum, not realizing I had moved on. I was speaking in high school health classes throughout New York City on Friday mornings, hoping to be the voice I needed to hear when I was 16 years old. As President of *Keep A Child Alive* on my campus, I helped raise funds to support orphanages and clinics on the African continent through art shows, featuring students and local artists. I decided to spend the remainder of the summer in Cape Coast, Ghana, working for a non-profit organization whose mission it was to educate students and young people about HIV prevention.

Here was this passion, staring me in the face and I hadn't realized how much I loved non-profit work. What would this mean in light of my long standing dream? I was going to be a doctor. There were hints that it wasn't working out--the blatant fail that was physics 101, for example. That said, I wasn't ready to give up.

Upon my return from Ghana, I started volunteering at the Harlem Hospital Center. One more line on the med school application and hopefully a letter of recommendation too. I reminded myself of that little motivator as I braced against the sardine-sensation that was the New York City subway at rush hour.

It was my third day working as a Spanish translator and the job was much more difficult than I anticipated.

When I walked through the door to the ER, my skin prickled. It's awfully quiet in here, I thought.

Marie, the nurse who trained me during my first two days, warned me about when the emergency room got too quiet. The eerie calm before the storm was to be feared not reveled in as much needed peace. She was one of the nice nurses, offering me her shoulder in her loving, mother-hen way, when she found me bawling in a stairwell one hour into my first shift.

The other nurses had harsh words regarding my regretful tough skin deficiency.

"You're never going to be a doctor if you can't check your emotions."

Through my tears, I stared at them in disbelief. I was supposed to be unaffected by telling a non-English speaking teenager that she is not only pregnant, but HIV positive? I would do no such thing. I bonded with Marie against the robo-nurses instantly.

"Hi, Marie," I smiled, picking up my pager from the nurse's station. "How are you today?"

"I'm well, lovely," she smiled back. "Little quiet today."

"I know!" I affirmed her suspicions. "I was just thinking that a second ago."

"Brace yourself, doll," she gave me a nod.

All these ER superstitions are a little too intense for me, I thought as I was making my way to the break room to wait for a doctor to page me if he needed my Spanish-speaking services.

150

I was walking by the automatic doors, when a huge black, SUV screeched to a halt and a lump came tumbling out the trunk's hatch.

"It's a body!" I heard Marie's voice.

"Oh my God! It's a man!" floated from somewhere else across the room.

Everyone with working legs ran to the door. But it wasn't a man. I saw his face. It was a child, a boy. No more than ten or eleven years old. He was bleeding from a gunshot wound in his shoulder and was screaming, spewing profanities, "Every one-uh ya'll! Stay the fuck away from me! Don't touch me!"

A team of physicians and nurses swarmed him anyway.

His wild eyes could no longer keep up the shield of faux machismo to cover his fear. His eyes locked with mine and he began to cry. He wasn't a miniature man dressed in baggy clothes, a cubic zirchonia medallion and a Yankees hat. He was a little boy, crying in terror. I took his hand just before he was whisked off to the operating room. I'm not sure why but I said, "I'm here. It's ok" and squeezed his hand. He squeezed back and someone yelled at me to get out of the way.

I immediately swung into action. My brain was moving faster than I could keep up with, where are his parents? It's a Thursday afternoon; why isn't he in school? Who was driving that truck? They obviously don't care about him. Why was he with them anyway?

I started writing out a few things I wanted to say to him when he woke up. "You deserve better than this," I began. I looked for resources and after school programs in the area with my cell phone. Marie came by to whisper in my ear, "Did you hear? The kid had a buncha baggies of coke in his pockets. He's probably a runner." I dropped my phone in shock. Looking over at the OR

door, I contemplated the trajectory of this young boy's life, which had catapulted his unconscious body onto a metal slab before puberty. Next to the doors was a huddle of doctors. That'll be me one day, I used to think when I saw the wrinkled white lab coats beneath young, tired faces. Today was different.
I was eavesdropping on their conversation, hoping to catch some tidbit about how Michael was doing. I never knew his real name, but I had always liked that name.

The white coats were talking about the reconstruction of blood vessels and damage to the shoulder socket. I realized I couldn't care any less about blood vessels if I tried. I was worried about Michael's wellbeing and his life outside the walls of that operating room. I followed their transfixed gazes through the window in the OR door and experienced none of their rapture.

It hit me like a slap in the face. I was no doctor.

The little girl with the plastic stethoscope who asked to listen to the heartbeat of everyone who crossed her dollhouse's doorframe would never become a surgeon.

Strangely enough, I didn't mourn the death of my dream. Instead, I was inspired, excited to know almost immediately that I didn't want to work within the healthcare system, but do everything within my power to change it, especially where the AIDS epidemic is concerned.

It appears I do not have the strength to witness human atrocities and remain stone-faced and coldhearted. The robo-nurses were right after all. I know now that I don't want that particular brand of strength.

I had always faced my life, trusting in my possession of a quiet strength. The kind of strength it takes to run a non-profit organization, to listen to the life stories of survivors. I took a survey of my life that day in Harlem Hospital Center and I realized I liked myself. I liked the choices I had made. I was brave enough to light a match when it was easier to curse the darkness. I was compassionate enough to hold a child's hand when he needed it the most. I already was who I had always wanted to be.

I tucked the little index card upon which I had scribbled down all my hopes for Michael into a plastic bag of his belongings and prayed that he would use it one day.

When I got back to my dorm, I gently placed my med school applications in the recycle bin down the hall. I wasn't throwing them away. My dreams would be made into something new. I smiled. I've always loved a good metaphor.

I was going to be something else, something different. And my heart, my desire to help people, would be the foundation of a beautiful life. I could just feel it.

Sixteen

I'm happy to report that my life is largely focused on my passions now. So while I've accepted my father for who he was, there are times I just wish I had a different dad—one who was good to my mother and could never dream of being away from his children for decades at a time. I could've used a good dad, but that wasn't my reality.

I find comfort in knowing I'm not alone. Actually, I don't believe anyone's pain is completely unique. Someone somewhere can relate to whatever you might be going through. And when someone is brave enough to step outside of ego, pride or shame to hear your story and say, "I've been there too," that's quite possibly one of the most beautiful parts of the human experience. I have yet to tell anyone about being sexually assaulted and heard a reply other than, "So was my college roommate." "So was my sister." Or simply, "Me too." As I've gotten older and braver in sharing my story, I've noticed more and more assault survivors could also relate to growing up in a dysfunctional, father-absent household.

With the divorce rate at over 50% in the United States, assault survivors are not the only ones who suffered because their Dad wasn't home everyday. Furthermore, I'm not the only one who is acknowledging the impact that empty chair at the dining room table is having either. The National Responsible Fatherhood Clearinghouse partnered with the Ad Council to create President Obama's public service announcement campaign to encourage fathers' involvement in their children's lives. Their website, fatherhood.gov, reports over 79% of Americans feel "the most significant family or social problem facing America is the physical absence of the father from the home." But the real question is, HOW is fatherlessness affecting and changing us, our society, our culture and in what ways? As the American family dissolves and absentee fathers become the majority or the norm, what does that mean for our future, for the way mothers will raise their sons, for the way daughters will choose their partners?

How can you raise a young man to uphold the ideal that a father is crucial, vital, irreplaceable in a child's life if he never had one? And how can you tell your fatherless daughter to choose wisely, to remember that she is choosing not just a partner for herself, but a hero for her children, no matter how unworthy he may be of that title? Do you go the "do as I say, not as I do" route? A quote by James Baldwin comes to mind for me here, "Children have never been very good at listening to their elders, but they have never failed to imitate them." And, alas, we are all imitators.

We do what we see and it becomes engrained. I remember learning about the Bobo Doll experiment in my behavioral psychology class, which tells a grim tale about learned behavior. Children witness a model aggressively attacking a Bobo doll, an inflatable punching-bag toy. 88% of the children imitated the aggressive behavior when presented with that same doll separate from the model. Eight months later, 40% of the same children reproduced the violent behavior observed in the experiment without prompting. Our children are watching us, doing what we do. Over the course of a generation, these children have grown into adults, watching and emulating each other.

Our culture has borne witness to a violent, aggressive attack on the institution of marriage. The media has even glorified it. Families are ripped apart every day, desecrating children's feelings of stability. Our parents got married for the wrong reasons and we can't help but imitate them. I didn't leave the boyfriend who called to yell at me in a jealous rage, "Where are you? Who are you with? What are you doing?" My parents had said far worse. I didn't know I had the right to say, "Dad, you can't leave. We need you here." Because my mother never did. Because American culture doesn't require or request the active involvement of our fathers. We aren't acknowledging how much we need them. So I'm asking, can we make a new standard? Can we make a new cast to mold our families after? We need a model worthy of emulation in order to reverse this cycle.

Unfortunately, it seems we've backed ourselves into a corner. If traditionally we've valued the mother's presence at home for child rearing purposes over the father's, it stands to reason that even if the family structure disintegrates, those values would stay the same. Active divorced dads mail their child support checks, send birthday cards, and in best case scenarios, see their children every other weekend. And it's still not enough.

Our culture is changing, pivoting around the central point of this trauma. Fatherhood.gov also reports, "...that the lack of a father in the home correlates closely with crime, educational and emotional problems, teenage pregnancy, and drug and alcohol abuse." People often blame parents when children or teens act out in these ways, which insinuates that family is the answer to these problems. But what kind of family?

Since the cookie-cutter 1950s American family is largely unrealistic in today's society—especially considering floating a family of four on one income is practically laughable in most cities—it's our responsibility to come up with another model. The haphazard mold we're using now has got to go. The revolving door of nannies, grandmothers, day cares, interspersed with once a month Dad visits that Mom doesn't want to be around for because then she'll be too pissed off and tired to do homework together is officially malfunctioning. The new mold must be deliberately considered before it is put into use.

Marriages don't always go the way we plan. Babies aren't always born at the most convenient time. My father used to warn me, "People don't plan to fail; people fail to plan." Assuming that no one wants to fail their children, parents have to make specific plans for their modern family's structure and ensure that both mother and father are having consistent quality time with their children—whether they're married, divorced or one-night-stand partners.

In my own fact finding quest, I was able to turn up a myriad of studies done regarding the impact of fatherlessness. The national Fatherhood Initiative organizes them by subject at fatherhood.org should anyone you know need to be reminded of how important their active involvement is in their child's life.

Most of the studies featured on the site yielded sad, but relatively unsurprising results to me. For example, children in father-absent homes are five times more likely to be poor. Fatherless children are twice as likely to drop out of school and a study of 13,986 women in prison showed that more than half grew up without their father. *Source cited in preface.*

However, there were two articles I found particularly interesting, so I will share the basics of them here. The first was published by Science Daily in June of 2007 under the title, "Fathers Have Great Impact on Their Children Even When Not At Home."

"Girls who had close, positive relationships with their parents during the first five years of life tended to experience relatively late puberty, compared to girls who had more distant relationships with their parents. More specifically, the researchers found that the quality of fathers' involvement with daughters was the most important feature of the early family environment in relation to the timing of the daughters' puberty.

Girls who enter puberty later generally had fathers who were active participants in care-giving, or had fathers who were supportive to the girls' mothers, and had positive relationships with their mothers. But it's the fathers' involvement, rather than the mothers', which seems to be paramount to the age of the girls' development. The researchers believe that girls have evolved to experience early socialization, with their "antennae" tuned to the fathers' role in the family (both in terms of father-daughter and father-mother relationships) and that girls may unconsciously adjust their timing of puberty based on their fathers' behavior.

The researchers found that girls raised in father - absent homes or dysfunctional father-present homes experienced relatively early pubertal timing.

They present several theories as to why this occurs. One biological explanation is that girls whose fathers are not present in the home may be exposed to other adult males - stepfathers or their mothers' boyfriends - and that exposure to pheromones produced by unrelated adult males accelerates female pubertal development. The flip side of that theory is that girls who live with their biological fathers in a positive environment are exposed to his pheromones and are inhibited from puberty, perhaps as a natural incest avoidance mechanism.

Girls who live with their fathers but have a cold or distant relationship with them would not be exposed to their fathers' pheromones as much as girls who have more interaction with their fathers, therefore causing the girls in the distant relationship to reach puberty earlier, the researchers hypothesize.

Perhaps most notable, the researchers say, is the important role fathers seem to play in their daughters' development, given that the quality of mothering is generally more closely associated with how children turn out than is the quality of fathering."

Penn State. "Fathers Have Great Impact On Their Children's Lives, Even When Not At Home." *ScienceDaily*, 13 Jun. 2007. Web. 6 Jun. 2011.

I found this absolutely fascinating. If a girl's father is a part of her life, his pheromones protect her from entering puberty early. If her father is absent, she enters puberty to attract the attention and hopefully, protection of a mate. The findings seem to imply that a woman is biologically made to secure the protection of man. That's a hot-button sentence and as a young woman who has come to value her independence, it almost makes me mad to type it. Yet, I can't help but hear it ring true, even in my own life. I began menstruating within the first year of my father's absence and went dashing off to find a boyfriend months before that. Girls are developing faster. But the question is, why?

The study of early on-set puberty has placed much of the blame on obesity, hormone-riddled fast food and sedentary lifestyles, but a study published by UC Berkeley in the journal of Adolescent Health in September of 2010 undermines that theory:

"The age at which girls are reaching puberty has been trending downward in recent decades, but much of the attention has focused on increased body weight as the primary culprit," said study lead author Julianna Deardorff, UC Berkeley assistant professor of maternal and child health. "While overweight and obesity alter the timing of girls' puberty, those factors don't explain all of the variance in pubertal timing. The results from our study suggest that familial and contextual factors -- independent of body mass index -- have an important effect on girls' pubertal timing.

....Contrary to what the researchers expected, the absence of a biologically related father was linked to earlier breast development for girls in higher income families—those having annual household incomes of $50,000 or more. Father absence predicted earlier onset of pubic hair development only in higher income African Americans families.

The mechanisms behind these findings are not entirely clear, the study authors said. Evolutionary biologists have theorized that the absence of a biological father may signal an unstable family environment, leading girls to enter puberty earlier.

....In some ways, our study raises more questions than it answers," said Deardorff. "It's definitely harder for people to wrap their minds around this than around the influence of body weight. But these findings get us away from assuming that there is a simple, clear path to the earlier onset of puberty."

University of California—Berkeley. "Father absence linked to earlier puberty among certain girls." *ScienceDaily*, 17 Sep. 2010.

Girls are entering puberty sooner, looking like women sooner. Lacking supportive family structures, they receive few of the tools they need to demand the respect their bodies deserve. How do you learn to value yourself if your parents don't show you how to?

Young men without fathers are more likely to be violent, engage in crime, struggle in school, and abuse drugs or alcohol. *Source cited in preface.* And the saga of broken families continues as these young men and women grow into adults and have their own children.

I'm not sure what we can do to show absent fathers how much their children need them. How essential they are to their children's everyday lives, development, identity and self-esteem formation. Perhaps we can begin by showing them their own broken children in hopes that a reaction is inspired in time for the children my generation is beginning to have.

I know some fathers are kept from their children and some blatantly can't afford the child support they're required to pay. Clearly, I don't mean to insult the men who are fighting to be with their children, but quite frankly, I don't want to celebrate them either. That's what a father should do. Unfortunately, there's a larger underlying issue in all this fatherhood absenteeism. Before the custody battle, before the embarrassing DNA testing, before the judge and the lawyers, there was a relationship or a marriage that shouldn't have happened. Not that any children should ever be regretted, but let's be honest, there's a reason people say to their soon-to-be divorced friends, "This will be so much easier. Thank God you guys didn't have any kids together."

For my peers who have yet to get married or have kids, I want to see us make better choices than our parents did, better partner selection in particular. I want us to bring babies into this world under the condition that a happy, honest, loving, supportive environment with two parents involved to the best of their abilities is ready and waiting their arrival.

I've heard others say, "Don't marry a man if you wouldn't be proud to have a son exactly like him" and "don't marry a woman who you find yourself trying to avoid, lie to or weasel away from just to have some alone time." I'd like to add, "And don't date them for too long either!" That's not the person who is meant for you and if you make a baby with the wrong person, you won't be the only one suffering. In many ways, this book is an argument to call the suffering parents endure post-breakup/post-divorce small by comparison to that of your abandoned or neglected children. People seem willing to accept that children suffer when their parents split up, but I wonder if they really know how much and how far-reaching the psychological ramifications really are.

I hope this book can be a wake-up call. We need to start making conscious efforts to get mentally healthy, choose good matches for ourselves and by any means necessary, foster healthy environments for children to be nurtured in to the best of our intentions and abilities. Because mothers can't do it all by themselves or rather, they shouldn't do it all by themselves. In their overworked, overstressed, overtired hands rest the psyches of the next generation.

Seventeen

I will always be an advocate for psychotherapy. However, I understand that not everyone can have the luxury of going to private sessions three times a week for free during college or taking a year off of high school to come back from the dead. I hope you'll forgive my obvious lack of academic qualifications to discuss the psychological intricacies associated with the impact of fatherlessness and allow me the chance to say that I think we're in trouble. Our girls, our boys, our families, our communities, our culture is in trouble. No, there isn't a hurricane coming and the terrorism warning color at JFK is still down at yellow for today.

This is something we actually have control over. This pain is one from which we can protect our children. So why aren't we doing it? Why aren't we encouraging and reminding our fathers that we need them? More than we need their money, we need their time, their input. We need to know they care so that we don't go out into the world, forming relationships off shaky foundations of self-worth.

Can you turn out to be an amazing and healthy woman or man all by yourself with the love and support of a single parent? Sure. Would it have been nice to have two active, loving parents? Of course, but we can't win 'em all. If you don't feel a particular parent's absence was detrimental to your upbringing, I certainly don't mean to take away from anyone's certainty of that. I wish, instead, to validate the young woman who never knew her father, but feels a void and wonders why she hasn't been single for longer than two weeks since she was thirteen. I wish to give the young man who has fallen into a depression after his abusive step-father has passed away some of the tools he can use to dig himself out of that hole. Ultimately, I wish to give the children of the fatherless tribe a place to migrate when they find themselves at a dead-end.

For me, the greatest weapon against depression was therapy. While the feedback I was given was especially helpful in the beginning, I think one of the most beneficial parts about therapy was simply being able to talk freely without fear of judgment. I spoke my peace and was able to sort out my jumbled thoughts just because I had said them out loud.

There are community centers, YMCA's, churches, and private non-profit organizations in cities all over the country who offer psychological services for free or at discounted rates.

We have to get it out, tell our stories. My therapist at Columbia once said that, "some people will almost completely stop emotional development at the point of trauma."

I was dating a twenty-four year old, trilingual, Wall Street banker at the time who threw massive, violent, breaking things fits if he didn't get his way. His father had committed suicide when he was five years old. Professionally, intellectually, physically, his development had sped right along. But emotionally, I was dating a very, very angry kindergartener. As much as I wanted to believe my therapist had brought this topic up because of him, I had no choice but to acknowledge that the way I was behaving in romantic relationships had a strong association to the relationship I had with my father.

This psychological entanglement isn't an active choice. You don't say to yourself, "Since my dad didn't show up to my eleventh birthday, I'm going to make sure I never trust any of my boyfriends. I'll check their cell phones when they're not looking and if I get caught, I'll be sure to find a way to blame

164

them for my invasive behavior and be overall bratty, immature, and unjustifiably jealous." Your irrationality will be none so clear. It happens slowly over the course of decades and you have to maintain a wide-eyed alertness to recognize where it might be affecting your everyday life and relationships.

The first thing you have to do is find that point or points of trauma. That letter writing tool made the trauma so clear to me. I've written a few dozen therapeutic letters over the years now: to my father, to the boy who raped me, to my racist elementary school principal who told me I would never "be anything," to friends, to Christine, to my mother.

I certainly don't have all the answers to healing psychological wounds our parents or others may have caused, but I know that therapy and acknowledgement of which weapons were used to create which wounds is a great place to start.

I'm not a guru or an expert or a doctor by any means. I don't mean to say, "Look at me! Follow my lead! I know exactly what I'm doing here!" On the contrary, I simply wish to share my truth, my way to wellness in hopes that it might help someone find their own. My journey was inspired to start upon realizing that the popular warning, "hurting people hurt people" was coming to life in my world. That scared me badly enough to want to change. I held a magnifying glass to my heart so I could find all the places that had been bruised. I didn't want to hurt my daughter with snide comments about her weight because I hadn't dealt with my anorexia. I didn't want to push my friends away because I hadn't dealt with the way Akin's health problems had molded the way I related to people. I didn't want to lose my husband because I was still seething-angry with my father for abandoning us. This method worked for me and it just might work for you too.

Still, it's not perfect. I have good days and I have bad days. Currently I'm coming to terms with the ways in which being assaulted permanently changed me. For me, that means shushing the monster inside me that's livid about the fact that rape ever occurs, let alone as often as it does. It stays quiet for longer periods of time now. I went almost a full year this time without having a breakdown, but there are triggers and when that bomb goes off, it's like my own emotional Hiroshima.

I find myself wondering, "How am I here again? Here in this all too-familiar despair...again." And the answer is usually because something's come up that I haven't dealt with yet. The triggers are fewer and farther between than they ever were, but they still exist. I saw a woman wearing a t-shirt that read, "I'm not the one who should be ashamed." I felt the pain registering with me. Suddenly, I was naked in Central Park. I don't think I had ever really addressed that emotion as valid for myself. Shame? Why should I feel that? I didn't do anything wrong. I was focused on being a survivor and not a victim. I wanted desperately to be strong. To be a success story. I hadn't stopped to address the feelings that were laced behind those piping hot showers.

If you choose to go to therapy, acceptance is a hot-button word you'll eventually hear and it's one you'll need to handle with care. You have to take a fine-tooth comb through the issue before you can accept it for all that it is. If you try to choke it down whole, it will come back again. And it won't be pretty.

Acceptance, in my mind, is a sweet ideal. Terrible things in life happen. Fortunately, they come to an end. But I don't have neutral feelings about what happened to me in that closet or the fact that my father swindled my mother out of every penny she ever earned. Those traumas took pieces of me, pieces that I can never get back. And I don't think that makes me crazy.

It's been ten years since I was raped and almost thirteen years since my father left for Nigeria. I can still express how much it hurts without my feelings being overdramatic, or an overreaction. I'm present. I'm acknowledging. I'm reacting. It's one of the best things I've done for myself in years: allowed myself to feel. To not be afraid of my own emotion. To pour my heart out of that bottle and let myself cry. Dismissing my pain was literally suffocating me. I had backed myself into a corner where I couldn't be myself because I didn't even know who that was anymore. I'm still piecing it together, my identity, that is. And I'm sort of madly in love with the patchwork, passionate, child-like, creative, loving, joyous, adventurous, loyal "self" that I'm building so far. I choose to live my life by a famous quote from George Bernard Shaw: "Life isn't about finding yourself. Life is about creating yourself."

One of the biggest pieces of that "patchwork self" is my love of travel. I do it as often as I can, wherever I can. Since I'm in the business of making sure I understand why I do the things I do, I had to wonder why I loved traveling so much. Seeing the beauty of the world, being exposed to other people and their traditions, cultures, foods, languages, religions, all fascinated me. But I think the real reason I love to travel is because it pushes your boundaries, pushes you to adapt. The principle at which you are unwilling to bend is who you are. I've learned more about myself abroad than I ever have in the States. I became a Christian in Jerusalem. I vowed never to let anyone abuse me again in any way in Cape Coast, Ghana. I decided I was ready to meet someone to fall in love with in Macchu Picchu. The places I've been have inspired me, required me to grow.

But none quite like Israel.

Sitting in an open field with a few sparse olive trees in Bethlehem, Palestine, I decided I would write this book.

Over the course of a few journal entries, the main topics I've covered were born. It's an insight to a deeply personal side of the way my brain works and how I finally stopped searching for my father.

167

Eighteen

11/21

Off to Israel! So, SO excited! Like, it hasn't fully set in yet that I'm leaving, but maybe now that I'm packing the click will happen. Alana is living there. Well, in Jerusalem technically. I'm flying into Tel Aviv. It'll be fun to see her. I haven't seen her since Bartending School a year ago!

11/22

Gila--is the name of the sweet elderly lady I met while waiting for my transfer in Milan. Most intense security EVER. She thought by telling the agent I was friends with her (she's an Israeli citizen) that it would make things easier for me. False. The agent asked 101 questions about how we knew each other, what our history was and I thought it was pretty obvious we were lying. The agent became bewildered and just asked us to please go through security separately. Fair enough. And we both made it to the Holy Land. I'm having lunch with Gila tomorrow at her house. Should be fun!

I'm in Tel Aviv now and my hotel is pretty cute. A little apartmentotel that kinda reminds me of a college dorm. I think it's all this cheap teak furniture.

I'm already totally infatuated with the sensation of this city. Everyone is so friendly and courteous and helpful. The men are respectful, but you know, still men. Naturally.

One of the main things I noticed is different is how freely people talk about God. So taboo to talk about God in the States. In a public place? You risk a stare down, a few glares, and definitely a handful of eye rolls that seem to say, ""Here we go again. Another right wing nut job." It still baffles me that people have a hard time understanding how I could be pro-choice, an advocate for gay rights, vote liberal and call myself a Christian.

Truth is, I'm not most Christians. I've had a hard time finding a church I feel comfortable in. If the ideology gets exclusionary or cult like, I'll make a break for it. And prosperity preaching? Also known as the idea that if you donate money to the pastor's "I need a BMW fund" then the good Lord will bless you? Don't get me started.

171

But people in Tel Aviv don't talk about God like Americans do: feisty and full of inappropriate political charges. They talk about Him like He's there. Like He's a part of life. Because He is.

A little boy on the bus ride to my hotel sat down next to his school mate and announced, "This morning, when I was eating my cereal, I feel like God was trying to tell me something..."

I overheard a woman wish her friend a safe journey home at the bus stop and she prayed a blessing over her, "May the Lord keep you until you arrive, my angel. Safe travels! Call me when you get home otherwise I'll be up praying all night!"

She was SHOUTING across the street. She didn't even think to feel awkward about such a statement. She was surrounded by Jews, varying from modern to Orthodox, devout Muslims, and a few Christians. They certainly didn't think of her as an extremist, zealot-weirdo and I realized, neither did I.

11/23

I saw Ambuyah right before I left and we talked about the phenomenon of singleness. It's a Friday night. There are two options for a single girl: singing Beyonce's 'Single Ladies' at the top of your lungs, toasting all your friends with a champagne glass or sulking in the kitchen eating an Entenmann's cake out of the box with no utensils, trying not to think about your ex. Further, whether or not you're enjoying the state of being single seems to determine who you attract. Whenever I've thought, "Oh, woe is me I'm single and so very lonely. I wish a decent man would come along and rescue me from this misery," I either don't get approached or only the garbage man 67 year old grandfather, dripping in gold chains is trying to holler at me from off the back of his truck. Meanwhile, as soon as I start thinking I'm going to focus on me. Do my own thing for a while. Suddenly, fantastic, eligible and not to mention beautiful men come flying out of the woodwork. Fascinating! What are we sending out energetically without even knowing it? Apparently, a lot more than we realize. I think it's more than "confidence is sexy." It's as if my mental health determined who I attracted. Sick me dated sick men and healthy me dated healthy men. Coincidence?

I set a dynamic with someone the moment I met them. Here are the boundaries. Here's what I'm willing to accept. When I was sick, I let them know right away that they could pretty much get away with anything as long as they made me feel loved. That's all I wanted. When I look back on meeting now ex-boyfriends, it was all there. The insecurity, the jealousy, the possessiveness. Ordering for me, asking how many people I've slept with, getting awkward when I told them where I went to school. They ain't nevah lied. I lied to myself. Ignoring red flags didn't make me a humanitarian or a loving, compassionate, supportive girlfriend; it made me a punching bag.

After my last often verbally abusive relationship culminated in a shove off a ledge that landed me face first in a pile of jagged rocks, in front of our closest friends, it seems some self-reflection is long overdue in this arena. Why do I keep attracting men who try to control me again? The Daddy abandonment complex, right? Alas, here it is again. I treat men like I did my father, being obedient, even servile. Basically, I've shown the men I've loved that I needed their superior guidance in my life, which I think made it completely impossible for them to view me as an equal.

In spite of my intelligence and laundry list of accomplishments, I still allowed myself to commit this incredulous disservice... against myself. Shockingly enough, I would then become upset when I felt unappreciated. It was positively maddening to me. Especially since they couldn't see that I was obviously the more "desirable candidate" in the relationship. That sounds conceited and terrible, but in reality, I deliberately chose those two men because I wanted to have the better background story. I didn't want to be the messed up one. I didn't want to be the one who needed help. I fell in love whole-heartedly believing in their potential and foolishly, egotistically believing in my own ability to help them get there.

I realize now that my two loves before therapy were with men who didn't exist. Their pure selves had been so distorted by abandonment, childhood traumas, neglect, verbal and physical abuse, that they couldn't function within a relationship or love me without hurting me, no matter how hard they tried.

Despite enduring their suffocating abuse, I believed that by loving them, investing in them, showing them the meaning of the magic word, consistency, I could HEAL them. I confused compassion with love and not to mention, severely overestimated myself. I'm not a psychologist, but I believed I could be a savior for them. I wanted to be the reason that they could believe in humanity, decency, and the true power of love in the face of all the ugliness they had been forced to witness. I would be a shining light and they would never abandon me for the darkness they once knew. Obviously. Of course, that's completely insane. For one main reason, I'm not God. But secondly, because, unfortunately, everything we've seen is inside of us and until we make deliberate decisions regarding how those impactful experiences, particularly the traumatic ones, will manifest themselves in our lives, emotional mayhem has the high potential to ensue.

Do I think that the ex who completely violated my privacy, read my emails, journal, and phone bills is a bad person? Or that the ex who pushed me is El Diablo personified? No, they did bad things and until they can address the underlying issues of insecurity and abandonment from their childhoods (just for starters), they will continue to hurt people like they did me.

I'm addressing my issues now because I don't ever want to end up in another abusive relationship. I want to acknowledge red flags for what they are and leave before it has to become a fiery, multiple car and train clusterf*ck for me to think, "Oh, maybe now I should leave him." I want my dignity back. I want to never again be "Captain Save-A-Bro!"

Sounds ridiculous, but I know so many women who do this...date and marry so dreadfully below them, it's almost laughable. To us, I'd like to say, here's the bottom line: he's not gonna change. He's not gonna wake up one day and realize that while you've been Super-Girl-ing it, he's been an ungrateful bum and wants to start all over, "get a job" and "treat you like you deserve to be treated." The best advice I could ever give any dater is to figure out what you want in a partner before you end up giggling like a hypnotized imbecile, drunk on two and half glasses of wine and the intoxication of their good smile.

Choosing a partner is one of the most important decisions you will make in your entire life and it deserves the utmost consideration, to say the least. What characteristics do you want? Get specific. Smart with a sense of humor isn't going to cut it. No one is perfect so figure out what flaws, insecurities, challenges you are willing to deal with. What are the absolute deal breakers? Meaning it doesn't matter if you're three dates in or you've been married for ten years with three kids, if _____ happens, you have to leave. No discussion.

When you meet a character who sparks your interest and you feel some chemistry, choose them for exactly who they are at that precise moment. Not who they could be one day and sure as hell not for who you want them to become. Cuz that's a fairytale that ain't gonna come true. In my experience, it will most likely end in depression, STD testing, trips to the ER, bouts of anorexia and then months of counseling. (See also: sheer and utter, all-encompassing misery. See also: not happily ever after...not even a little bit.)

Keep your ears and eyes open. Make sure you're not filling in blanks with characteristics about them you're assuming or outright inventing. When someone shows you who they are, believe them.

Wanna jump the broom? Great! Hold on to your honey and go for a premarital counseling ride first. Make sure you're on the same page. About finances, about spending habits, where you want to live, about kids, how you want them to be raised and disciplined, about what you want from your partner, emotionally, physically, about expectations, time spent with in laws, household chores, religion and faith, who's making dinner, about credit, about sex, about vacations, about your future goals and dreams, as individuals and as a couple. It'll probably be a lot of work. But it will give your relationship a foundation to build from and provide the two of you with a blueprint to follow so neither of you is surprised when unexpressed expectations don't match reality. Your partner's not a mind reader and you're not a magician. So get real before you get married. It'll make for a smoother ride and your children will thank you.

With this in mind, here are my illustrious plans for the impending year.

-Do the things I love to do: travel, write, spend time with my friends and family. Eat.
-Work Out (note separation from "the things I love" category)
-Never stop reading
-Start writing
-Date as I see fit
-Keep eyes open for red flags. know what I want. know what I don't want.
-Knock a few items off the "To Do B4 40" list
-Enjoy myself
-Take care of myself
-Be faithful to what I know is true

PS I love that I'm writing this in Israel.

11/24

Wow... I could live here....

I've never felt that way about a place I've traveled. Paris? But it wasn't like this. Funny how love is. You think you love someone or something, until you meet true love and you realize how pitifully the former paramour now pales in comparison.

I can't wait to get to Jerusalem tomorrow. I want to go to the Holy Wall and put my prayers in the cracks. I've been writing them for weeks now. I hope there's enough space for all of mine!

I find it interesting that as soon as I have a free moment to myself, to breathe, to relax, the very first thing I want to do is write. Well, eat and write. At the same time. I'm a writer, I suppose. How do I know? I imagine it must be a bit like finding "the one." It's effortless to be with them and when you are, you find yourself simultaneously at peace and inspired to be the best version of yourself that you can be.

Note: do research on literary agencies
possible themes: something about fathers, their importance.

11/25

Woke up so heinously late today. It's like almost 3pm.

Oh jet lag...

I'm sitting out at the beach now. It's so gorgeous and clear. The water feels so pure. Tomorrow I'll wake up early enough to come to the beach before the day is halfway through.

So I met a guy on the beach and he was well, interesting, I guess is the word. But I actually mean it. I hung on his every word. He told me about his life and his extreme reactions to loss (of love, of finances, of innocence). He was fascinating and I felt like taking notes half the time he spoke. But something was off. Every time he touched me I felt a singe. Like it nearly hurt. Even though he was gentle and sweet, I found myself weaseling away from his touch. His name was Josef and he was in disturbingly good shape for having more salt than pepper in his tousled gray hair. I would guess he was in his late 40s. I never asked even though I spent over twelve hours with him. It just wasn't relevant.

I liked listening to him. Which is rare for me. Usually a guy on the street who I can tell was looking at my butt when I walked by has nothing of interest to say. It probably helped his cause that he's going on fifty.

We talked for hours. A few things I remember:

He told me that there are three keys to freedom in life: the keys to your car, your passport, and the keys to your heart. So long as you remain in the possession of those three things you can always achieve freedom.

181

He also told me about my "hamsa"--this beautiful necklace I bought in the marketplace right before I met Josef. It's an ornate silver design in the shape of a hand. It's meant to symbolize the hand of God. For protection. It's also the way rabbis hold their hand when they give blessings. However, it's not specifically Jewish. It originated from a time when nomads were roaming what would eventually become Israel. I really love it. It feels powerful to me. You know how when you wear something for a long time, like a ring or watch, sooner or later you forget you have it on? Well for some strange reason that's not happening with my "hamsa." I'm almost constantly aware of it. And I find myself smiling to myself a lot. Just walking down the road.

11/26

Today was a bit of a bust. Woke up at 4pm. Walked almost the whole of Dizengoff Street. Bought a beautiful blue cape, which I adore. It has a bright yellow lining. I think I'm learning how to be happy on this trip.

I'm doing what I want to do when I want to do it. Eating. Talking to strangers. Laughing by myself. And even though I bought my cape I feel strangely cured of my previously insatiable desire for clothes, shoes, girly crap. It suddenly seems...I have enough. I had been playing this crazy game in which I wanted to be the exception to the rule. I imagine it is very rare that a brown girl in $400 boots and a silk cape walks into your boutique on Columbus Avenue and 70-whatever Street. It's like you don't quite know what to make of me right? I don't look like anyone you know so you actually think it's appropriate to say, "Excuse me, what are you?" All of your preselected racist categorizations about class and my ability to afford your overpriced leather and lace are ringing like church bells in your head. "What is she doing in here?" I could practically hear you thinking. And it drove me insane. I would pick out expensive blouses I almost didn't even want just to spite the sales girls...and my credit. (Oops. I guess I do care what people think after all.)

I did figure out that even though I've acquired all these beautiful things I feel a negativity surrounding it. Guilt for the excess and the defeatism for never receiving the shocked, "Wow! I totally underestimated you and your people! I'm going to start giving equal and fair customer service to all! From this day forth!" speech. Maybe because it was all in my head and I was projecting my own social discomfort on to purposefully aloof (a.k.a dizzy from bulimia) failed models who dejectedly work in NYC retail.

Option B is the retail therapy I self-prescribed after Akin's heart attack and the break up had run its course. (I had high hopes for that relationship. Maybe he was sent to me to be the last one I would try to save. So that I would have some energy left to save myself.)

I've found a better way to channel the energy and all that danged money I've been spending on keeping the boutiques on Columbus afloat. The answer very clearly to me now is travel. I must do it as often as humanly possible.

I have so much work to do this year. Spiritually and mentally. I imagine celibacy and saving money for travel will block two of the major channels that had previously been letting in so much hurt, preoccupation and well, chaos, into my life.

I'm too highly sensitive of a person to separate sex from love. In that first long relationship after the assault, I did it in hopes that I could feel something. I thought if we had sex then I would love him. I think I believed I could use sex to jar me out that numb state I was in so that I could feel...anything. Even if it was pain.

I know I'll never be in that dark of a place again. I know where to go, who to call, and what to say if I need help now. But I think I just needed something to hold on to, something that was standing still in all that swirling madness. I needed to believe that God was real and that He hadn't given up on me. That it wasn't too late for me.

When I went to Bethlehem today, I have to say, I've never felt more sure. That He's alive. In me. In my friends. In my siblings. In my mom. In my Aunt V. In my nephew's laughter. In a strangers kindness. In the ocean, animals, the mountains, He's everywhere I look.

184

I feel a constant certainty and unwavering joy about that. Not an elated, jumping up and down hyperactive joy. More like a serene comfort. Like standing on solid ground after a downhill, unstable rocky hike that you kept losing your footing on and landing on your ass when you thought that ledge was solid.

Feels good to be on the ground. To appreciate simplicity. I feel so humbly grateful.

Thinking back to earlier today when I was wandering through a bunch of art galleries on Gordon St. on my way down to the Sea (that's what people call it here). There were these black and white rather crude, almost elementary looking paintings of characters that were performing circus acts but were dressed as ordinary people. One that stood out to me was called "Urban Acrobat." It was a shadowy, faceless man in a suit and tie that was fitted to his body like a leotard. He was juggling three plates, losing his balance slightly and walking heel to toe along a tightrope that was actually just a crack in the sidewalk.

Art is, of course, subject to interpretation and that's one of the things I love about it. To me, it seemed to say that it's ok to stop the juggling act, to fall off the tightrope. You look like a clown trying to keep all that up, anyway. The drop to the floor below, to your death, is all in your head. (He's already on the sidewalk.) Society tells us we have to do x+y+z to have a successful life, but what measures are they using to define success? Does success = happiness at the end of this equation? Not necessarily. So stop doing what you think you're supposed to be doing and figure out what you actually want to do.

God bless Columbia because one of the things I actually remember from all the Greek myth and philosophy is a particularly interesting funeral tradition. When a man passed away, they didn't read long accounts of life and his accomplishments. They asked one relatively simple question, "Did he have passion?" Which seems to suggest that if the answer was "yes," regardless of whether that passion was for the law or for needlepoint stitching, then his life was worth living.

I think it's also important to be unafraid of a longer answer to that question for myself. I know I want to write, help change health care in this country, travel ceaselessly, have my own web travel show, learn photography, design a few shirts for mixed kids, create a website where mixed kids can talk to each other, patent my baby product invention, maybe get my Ph.D. in psychology—so far. I've got a lot to do in this lifetime. Why people feel like they have to do one thing for the rest of their lives completely flabbergasts me. I might even teach for a while. Who knows? I just want to be open to wherever God wants to take me. I would really like to invest more time in my writing.

I feel this calling on my heart to write this book. I've started jotting down chapter ideas and it's like pouring out of me. I feel like I was meant to do this. At the end of the day, I want my story to be to others what I so desperately needed: to know I wasn't fighting this battle all by myself.

I was actually writing the first chapter by the beach when Josef walked up to me and put a little twist on a pretty common phrase. Foreigners do it all the time and it's endearing to me. My dad used to say, "Let's not beat the bushes." Instead of "Let's not beat around the bush." I never corrected him because it was kinda cute. Josef said, "I didn't want to disturb you in case you were cleaning your mind." I opened my mouth to make the slight adjustment, but found myself considering the new implications. I liked it better that way, I realized. Instead of clearing your head to achieve nothingness, I was "cleaning" in there. To achieve order. To organize and make sense of *all that's been thrown in there as helter-skelter stimulus.*

Thanks, Josef. I'll keep that one.

I think I figured out what a partner is supposed to do. Well actually, mostly I just see how wrong I had it before. My boyfriend will be a man. Not a super-hero rescuer and certainly not my savior, protector, redeemer, fulfiller, or maker. God is love so it got a little blurry for me.

I want to deliberately choose my interactions with my boyfriend. Not feel controlled by the blueprint my childhood has laid out for me to repeat. I want to love intentionally and purposefully. I want to choose my life and a life together with someone.

I don't want to end up in some too expensive apartment I hate because we ran out of time and the baby we didn't plan is coming and we're not married and now he's staying out late drinking and my job doesn't offer paid maternity leave and and and… it's a slippery slope that I want to make damn sure I avoid. For the sake of my sanity and the love we'll share. For the sake of our children and the environment they deserve to be nurtured in.

I think being given the gift of a life is like being entrusted with an angel. Should I decide to have children, I don't plan on taking that duty lightly.

Ok bedtime. Big day tomorrow.

11/27

I finished the first three chapters of the book. I think I'm going to call it "In Search of My Father." That feeling, that phrase, that sentiment has fueled my very existence. My adolescence and identity were molded around those words. I was searching for my father in my every interaction, in my every motion. Begging for validation, acknowledgment, I was nothing without that search. I see it in other people too. They're looking for the same promise of solidity and permanence that I was. It's like trying to find something to hold on to that's true. That's yours. That no one can take from you. And it can be a harrowing, ceaseless search without help.

I spent the day in the Old City of Jerusalem with Alana and her family friend, Ari who's staying at the Old City Yeshiva. I saw Mt. Zion and the Mountain of Olives from their rooftop. It was one of the most beautiful things I've ever seen.

When we hunched over into the highly secured, tiny crawl space where Christ is reportedly buried, I felt extremely skeptical at first. Christ's tomb? How on earth could anyone know that for certain? I've never even heard about this and I was a Catholic for the first twelve years of my life. Like, an every Sunday Catholic and they made it sound like Italy was the center of the universe. I bowed my head out of respect, but kept an eye out for the inevitable donation box.

I took in the simplicity of the carved rock, the stalagmite formations created by thousands of candles, and the roses on the ground. It was lovely. My heart softened. And then suddenly, the earth was moving. I reached out for the wall to steady myself and I was surprised to discover that I wasn't scared. I closed my eyes and felt this incredible force, washing up and down the walls of the tomb like waves. I felt alight, afloat, weightless. It was swirling around me and when I opened my eyes I half expected to see Walt Disney-style fairy dust sparkling around the room, surrounding me. My body felt like it was sparkling from within, like my cells were crystals bursting up from the prehistoric cave floors in my organs. For a moment, I didn't feel human. I thought to myself, incredulously, "What is this?"

And I felt something inside me say, "You wanted to know if I was real. If I was with you. I am your Father and I am always with you. Never forget this day. It is the day that I have touched you."

It felt like flowers opening down my sternum and water running over my sacrum. Words fail me here, but it felt unearthly. I have no idea exactly what happened or how long I stood there. But I do know that I'll never doubt whether or not God exists again.

Alana had been with me the entire time and I had practically forgotten anyone else was in there.

"Whoa," she said, breathlessly. "What was that?"

She put her hand over her heart.

"I... I...." I struggled to find the words. "It was God."

Well, I'm not really a believer," Alana said, but I don't think anyone could deny that. It was like the ... that's what people mean when they say the Holy Spirit."

I smiled.

As we walked out of the Old City, I felt like a totally different person. My body felt different. My skin felt different. I felt the ground beneath my feet in a new way. As time went on, I realized the foods I craved were totally different. The way I carried myself, the way I held my face was different. I'm going to donate half my clothes to Good Will when I get home because those clothes seem to belong to a different girl.

I looked at myself in the mirror at Alana's house and remembered the light I saw being sucked out of my pupils that night as I held the counter in Ryan's mother's bathroom in a futile attempt to fight the force of depression on my own. The ice melted off that teenager, frozen in the airport, hugging her daddy goodbye. She could walk again. I saw that broken girl inside me, but the dichotomy was too great to be reconciled. I simply wasn't her anymore. Where I had been defined by darkness, there was now light.

My faith is a choice. I can't give you a scientific equation to prove anything to you. I just know what I feel in my heart is true. Faith is a personal journey and I would never try to rush anyone along in theirs. I'll leave the judgment up to someone else. I remember how much it hurt to receive cold looks and harsh words when I so desperately needed compassion and a soft place to land. Simply put, that's a kind of karma I don't want to know.

I think I learned to stop being afraid I was going to mess my life up and to trust that I know how to get all the answers I need. In Israel, I found peace. With myself, with who I am, with who I was.

Later that afternoon, Alana and I went to the Western Wall and I brought this journal so I could take the prayers I had written and slip them into the cracks. There were so many people and so many prayers in the wall. You could tell some had been there a very long time. I stood beside men, women, children, a group of elderly veiled widows, Jews, Muslims, Christians, a tiny Buddhist Monk and at first I just listened as all the different languages swirled together, crying out to God. It was a breathtaking spiritual experience. People from all over the world with different ideologies and customs had come together in the name of prayer. Coexistence was possible.

I tore the pages out of this journal, all the prayers I had written. I read a few entries more closely and I realized, He's who I have always been writing to, who I have always been looking for. I hugged my journal to my chest. I felt found.

I placed my prayers delicately around the others. One for my mom, Akin, for each of my sisters, for my Shannon, my dad, for the continent of Africa, for the President of the United States, for everyone who's been sexually assaulted, for all the single moms, for all the children who will go to sleep afraid tonight, for the scientists working on a cure for HIV, and lastly, for everyone who doesn't know that they have a Father in You, too.

The last one read:

To my fellow members of the fatherless tribe, my brothers and sisters, my heart,

I am holding us up today and as always I'm holding you close to my heart. My prayer for us this day and every day is for a sense of fulfillment--for confidence and enjoyment in all that makes us special to others and a deep abiding peace within that you ARE.

I'm praying for our renewal, our revival, our healing and cleansing. My beautiful family, today, like a phoenix we will rise again glorious and victorious reborn to reclaim all that is rightfully, earnestly ours.

When King Nebecenezzer ordered Shadrach, Meschach, and

Adednego bound, tied and thrown into the furnace for refusing to worship a worldly statue, he later found them walking around in the flames with a fourth accompanier, untouched, unhurt, without even the smell of fire on them. It is proclaimed then: all that our sufferings have damaged, corroded, viciously burnt down and destroyed will ONLY be that which was binding us.

Not even the hairs on our heads will be singed to provide others evidence of our suffering. We are not damaged. We are not hopeless. We are not too crippled by our trauma to walk, to love, to live. On the contrary, when we decide to let go, we will be free, free and accompanied by angels.

I pray for our boundless freedom that allows us the heavenly space to dance, sing, play, laugh, be with our family and friends, find our passions, nurture the animals and land around us, make art, support any cause our heart is called to, fall in love, see the world, and simply be free to be as we are, here on earth: angelic.

I pray that our smiles from this day forth will be untainted by past sorrows.

I pray for love in its purest form virtually unrecognizable to us, not even as a mere shadow of any love we have ever been shown before.

I pray for us unadulterated perfect gentle sunshine, for warmth and tenderness in simple moments. I pray for us peace, wisdom and grace. And the all encompassing comfort of knowing we are never alone and we are not Fatherless.

I love you all.

Finding Nemo © Jonathan Walton
Written by my friend and colleague, poet and performer: Jonathan
Walton

You ever seen Finding Nemo?
You know the Pixar flick about 2 clownfish
a father, Marlon, stuck in the ocean trying to find his son
you know the one with one fin
I'm watching the scene
where they're riding the East Austrailian current or the EAC
and the sea turtles are like dude, and this one's like dude...
and he intro's his son and he said dude too.
Now the turtle's son gets pulled out by the tide they're riding
and Nemo's dad wants to save his life
but the turtle's dad lets him swim
giving his son the chance to try
a second passes and I reckon
the baby turtle gained his senses
because 2 seconds later
he and his father were like duuuude and celebrating.
Fast forward two scenes
and Nemo's hearing his father's story
of how he fought three sharks
and a forest of jellyfish, all to save his boy
Nothing was going to stop him
fear was something he didn't know
because there isn't a length long enough to measure
the lengths that he would go...
and Nemo smiled as he heard this and
for some reason tears filled my eyes
and as the story grew more elaborate
I began to cry
Nemo's father didn't just care

he cared to the point of not caring about himself
he would find his first and only born
if it meant that he would first find death
and that's what I never had
a father, a pop or dad
that man that would go to the ends of the earth
to see that I became a high school grad
make sure that I knew the difference between a Phillips head and one
that was flat
to tell me if I wanted it straight across or taped out in the back
I cried because Nemo had a father struggling to find him
and I only had a man striving to deny me
I cried a cry of neglect, a cry of abandonment
saying my own Abba Abba Nada sabachtani
And then I heard a voice
I was there when you wrote your first poem
there for your first bike ride
there when you lost your first tooth
and the first time you tried to drive
there when you got accepted to college
there when you gave your first speech
there when you decided to pick up your cross and follow me
I was proud of you in gym class
and art class and science
you've been looking for me from the beginning
and since the beginning, it was my desire for you to find Me.
I am your father in heaven and I knit you together in the womb
shaped you in my own image and trust that I love you
More than you can imagine, more than you will ever know
trying to wrap your mind around my love
is like shooting an arrow without a bow
for my love is boundless, limitless, eternal and everlasting
and my peace from that love all-encompassing and all-surpassing

196

I love you, son and that love is the truest truth
I count you precious and call you mine
and all I have, I give to you
the first fruits of the spirit
peace, joy, self-control
kindness, faith,
from my heart to yours
patience, kindness, meekness
take them with blessed assurance
that I am here and forever will be
your Heavenly Father
providing all you will ever need.
I felt better than Nemo
because this was life, not a cartoon
and this story didn't end with a whale and Dori
but it's still being written every time
I take the stage and a crowd is before me
because I know my father is watching.

Dear Mom,

This book begins in a window of time during which you and I were very far apart. I am so proud of how far we've come since those years and how much work we have both done to make our relationship what it is today. Thank you for all your love and support. Thank you for every swim meet, basketball game, flute recital, open house, pageant, and graduation. Thank you for investing in me. I am who I am, where I am, because of that. Thank you for sharing with me your loves of travel and photography; they became my own. Thank you for flying across the world to be my number one fan. Thank you for inspiring me, for the sacrifices you made for Akin and me. Thank you for teaching me that it was better to love others then myself; to be smart rather than pretty; generous rather than wealthy. Thank you for showing me how to give with a pure heart. I have treasured these gifts, passed them on to others and one day, I will give them to my own children.

I love you and I'm sorry that I didn't know better than to believe Daddy's lies at the time, but I was just a child. I know the truth now and I am grateful to have had a mother who loved me enough to put me first when I needed her the most. Thank you for hearing my cry.

The blog associated with this book where you can contribute your own letter to your father is,

www.Shadé ashani.tumblr.com

The author is also currently working on a t-shirt line and social network site for people of multiple heritages.

www.mixedthemovement.com

Resources

EFT (Emotional Freedom Techniques) Self-help stress relief
www.eftuniverse.com or www.emofree.com

The Rape Treatment Center of Santa Monica
Santa Monica-UCLA Medical Center 1250 Sixteenth Street Santa
Monica, California 90404
(310) 319-4000
www.911rape.com

Rape, Abuse & Incest National Network www.rainn.org
You can access their online hotline to chat with a counselor live,
or find resources near you, get help, or get involved with the
cause.

To find services for rape survivors in your area, call RAINN at 1-
800-656-HOPE.

If you're looking for discounted counseling in your area, call
local therapists, churches, YWCA or YMCA, and just ask!

17324303R00109

Made in the USA
Charleston, SC
06 February 2013